CELIBACY

CELIBACY

BY E. SCHILLEBEECKX, O.P. «

Translated by C. A. L. Jarrott

SHEED AND WARD · NEW YORK

Originally published as *Het ambts-celibaat in de branding,*
Uitgeverij H. Nelissen, Bilthoven (1966).

Published in England under the title *Clerical Celibacy
Under Fire.*

Nihil obstat: Lionel Swain STL LSS

Imprimatur: ✣ Patrick Casey, Vicar General

Westminster, 14 November 1967

*The Nihil obstat and Imprimatur are a declaration that a book
or pamphlet is considered to be free from doctrinal or moral
error. It is not implied that those who have granted the Nihil
obstat and Imprimatur agree with the contents, opinions, or
statements expressed.*

Library of Congress Catalog Card Number 68–13845

Manufactured in the United States of America

CONTENTS

Contents   7

CELIBACY

INTRODUCTION

THE PROBLEM PRESENTED: A DEMAND
FOR A NEW IMAGE OF THE PRIESTHOOD

With the demand for a new image of the priesthood, particularly in connection with the renewal of seminary training, the question of celibacy is constantly present, even if
it is not explicitly mentioned. The problem of clerical
celibacy today therefore invites us to make a critical appraisal of this form of life within the church.

The renewed awareness of man's historicity in his "having to be" as man-in-the-world has brought to the fore the
tremendous significance of the future dimension of our
human life. Everywhere the hermeneutical problem keeps
cropping up, in our biblical studies, theological speculations,
and in every reflection upon the structures of the church.
For human experience not only happens temporally; it also
includes an awareness of time. Experienced time is the time
which the human subject perceives as a being-in-the-world,
but in his *awareness* of time man transcends it, even though
he cannot conquer it, or, as it were, put himself outside it.
The course of our present life as it goes towards the future
from out of the past has become the central problem in the
world as well as the church. Becoming aware of this dimen-

sion *is* the present crisis, in the life of the church as well as in the economic, social, and political life of the world. It is obvious that our ideas of man, the world, and God that provided the basis for the structures, forms, and expressions of the past have been fundamentally altered. But the forms and structures have remained; thus they have become all but incomprehensible and no longer viable for us. Insecurity prevails everywhere.

This is the context of the hermeneutic problem. First, we will try to understand these forms and structures which have been handed down to us in terms of the past and the motives that gave rise to them. But, realising that we too stand within history as creatures who can transcend our own experience of time in looking towards the past as well as toward the great future before us, we are ready to pull down the structures that are no longer relevant. This is not to be done by means of a first phase of destruction ("demythologising") and a second phase of restoration; instead, by reinterpreting from the past we bring the future into the present. The "destructive" movement is impossible without at least an implicit vision of the future and a desire for it; if this were not the case it would be pure nihilism: revolutionary without any new values, which is the destruction of every "true revolution." The truth lies before us, in the future. But we, too, are men who come from the past, a past that was once a future for others, and therefore contains realised truth and values for us.

This critical approach therefore should not make us forget a fundamental fact: the implicit trans-historical moment

within history itself, and also within the actual experience
of faith. Deeper than any changing idea of man, the world,
and God (three correlative moments of a single attitude
toward life), although inextricably bound to it, lies the
unspoken religious experience which is God's inner word
to man's heart: the intuition of faith which strives for
expression. The present question, whether celibacy "for the
sake of the kingdom of heaven" (Mt 19:12)[1] does not become irrelevant with the recognition of the value of secular
realities, of marriage and sexuality, is therefore fundamentally ambiguous. It overlooks at the outset the possibility of
a pre-reflective conviction of faith (that is, a conviction
that exists before any consciously reasoned development of
it), of a knowledge already possessed that looks for a way
to express itself. The breakdown of the arguments for the
Christian significance of celibacy that had been developed
in the past undoubtedly destroys their validity, and rightly
so. But this does not in itself imply that thereby a pre-
reflective intuition of faith which possibly was present in
them is also destroyed or declared irrelevant. From our
present-day human and Christian situation we can reach
the conviction (as our analysis will show) that the reasoned
expressions or motives for religious celibacy that have been
handed down to us are no longer applicable; but this means
only that the truly present intuition of faith came to be

[1] *The Holy Bible, Revised Standard Version,* New York, Nelson, 1946,
1952. All scriptural quotations in this book are from this version, copy-
righted 1946 and 1952 by the Division of Christian Education of the
National Council of Churches.

mistakenly formulated and was transmitted with insufficient care. The same intuition of faith propels us towards a new clarification of these convictions present in our own experience in a way that will be suited to our own times. It is noteworthy that while the traditional arguments and motives are now in crisis on the Catholic side, the new idea of man developing in our times reveals a rediscovery of Christian celibacy on the Protestant side.

There is a real danger of a re-emergence of rationalism, of identifying human awareness with our reflective systematisation of the content of consciousness. This restriction of consciousness becomes all the more precarious, dangerous, and critical if it concerns a mystery of the Christian faith. Naturally, a mystery of faith can never be fully conceptualised; the conceptualisation of it is even of a different order from the philosophical. Within the deposit of faith, the mystery becomes approachable for us in our human demand for rationality only by way of arguments of congruence, "rationes convenientiae." In other words, looking with humility for the inner coherence of the mysteries of faith, we can make the biblical belief in celibacy "for the sake of the kingdom of God" inwardly meaningful and to some extent comprehensible. We can also try in this way to distinguish, in the first instance, whether, in the Bible, this is really a conviction of faith or just a notion derived from an outdated concept of man and the world. By definition, we cannot wholly justify Christian celibacy in rational terms (if it is a datum of faith), any more than we can rationally justify our act of faith itself. And yet we do not call this act of faith humanly unreasonable; it can be morally justified. Just because the very heart of Christian celibacy is surrender in faith, people in past times or future times can never expect to reach a rationally compelling proof of its excellence for salvation, for Christians in general and for church officials in particular. The reflective argumentation for the significance of celibacy for salvation belongs to what moderns call *la raison élargie*, that is, to that kind of knowing in which we can recognise something as true without being able to justify it in rational terms. But first we have to establish carefully that a real and authentic intuition of faith essentially underlies all these reflective arguments, good or bad—an insight striving to express itself successfully and meaningfully. Although the essentials lie in the experience itself and not in the motivations given for it upon reflection, nevertheless it is only in the meaningful expression of this experience that religious celibacy becomes entirely livable in a human way. With the destruction of the traditional arguments, many people now feel that the reality of religious celibacy itself is slipping out from under their feet, and this fact indicates that a successful and meaningful expression of it for today's world has not yet been found. This little book is an effort in that direction.

In a concise survey I will list and interpret the reasons given in the church's history for the first spontaneous practice of celibacy. That will direct our attention to two aspects already mentioned: on the one hand, the presence of an authentic religious intuition, and on the other hand, the relative, historically limited and outdated nature of its thematic expression. It is striking that each period of more intense experience of the ideal of "lifelong virginity" led to a renewed theological consideration; and on the other hand that again and again in the history of the church, a fundamental doubt has arisen concerning the formulation of celibacy in the Latin church (the law of celibacy). We should pay close attention to the significance of both reactions. In this stage of the analysis I still remain uncommitted to whatever the end result of the study may be. I am not defending any thesis but only searching freely, listening to the life of the church as it flows on under the guidance of holy scripture.

I »
Clerical Celibacy
in the Life and
Understanding of
the Church

1

THE CONNECTION BETWEEN CELIBACY AND OFFICE IN THE HISTORY OF THE CHURCH

"PRIEST" AND FAMILY IN APOSTOLIC TIMES

"We have no temples and no altars," wrote Minucius Felix at the end of the second century.[1] The "church" or community of the faithful gathered together at the homes of hospitable Christians (see, for example, Acts 20:20–21; 11: 15; 16:12–15, 19–34; 18:18). The Apostolic Letters ask hospitality especially from "presbyters" and "bishops" (1 Tim 3:2; Tit 1:7–9). This is not just the solicitous reception of a Christian on a journey; above all, they must receive the community at their homes for their assemblies. This requires an especially considerate attitude on the part of the host. Thus in the early days of Christianity, the "church" was closely bound up with the *family*. As yet there was not, as in later times, a *domus ecclesiae*—that is, there was no house set aside by a rich Christian to serve solely as a gathering place for the faithful—and of course the "basilica" was still a long way off. The ministry of the

[1] Octavius, 32; *Corpus Scriptorum Ecclesiasticorum Latinorum* (CSEL) II, 45.

word, the breaking of bread, and the many forms of charismatic service took place at home.

This connection between family life and church life was so close that people expected their church officials to have the same qualities as a good head of a family, who, in union with his wife, knew how to keep his household in good order: "A leader in the community . . . must be the husband of one wife . . ." someone who administered his own house well and kept his children well disciplined, with due regard for human dignity. If a person did not know how to manage his own household, how could he take responsibility for the household of God? (1 Tim 3:2, 4–5; 3:12; Tit 1:6–9.) The "elders" were thus in fact wise heads of families who at the same time held principal offices in the church. It was required of these "priests" and deacons that they have an undivided love for their wives: each must be "husband of one wife" (1 Tim 3:2, 12; 2 Tim 2:24; Tit 1:6). People have pondered over the meaning of these words. Some have thought that they had some connection with polygamy, but the context and the custom of the Jews at this time does not allow this interpretation. Catholic tradition has understood the text as a precept of the church leaders not to marry again after their first wife dies.

Modern exegetes, including Catholics, translate it as follows: "cling undividedly to one wife," as one might say, "homo unius libri," a man who swears by one book. Indeed, scholars have found monument inscriptions from those times (among both Jews and heathens) which state the following in praise of the deceased: "the husband of one wife" —whereas we would say on our memorials: "he loved his wife." The context seems to support this exegesis: such a man must love his wife with an undivided love, govern his children well, and be a good administrator of his own household. The whole passage moreover treats of the good qualities that a leader must have, and of the defects that impair his work, but lays down no laws for the future. This exegesis is not only possible, but highly probable, even though church tradition since patristic times has read this text to mean that a "priest" and deacon might not remarry or be married for the second time, viz: when they are ordained.

The image of a church official in apostolic times is thus that of a married, mature man, who as a father gives an example of good family government, and along with all these qualities of leadership has been chosen to be "deacon," "priest," "bishop," or other functionary within the church. There is no indication of any rejection of woman or of sexuality in connection with the priesthood. Church life and family life (in the broad sense of the word) are carried on in the same "profane" environment; that of the Christian home with wide-open doors.

All this concerns leaders of local churches. But what was the situation among the apostles themselves, who had left everything and followed Christ?

A BIBLICAL FACT: "EXISTENTIAL
INABILITY TO DO OTHERWISE"

"There are eunuchs for the sake of the kingdom of heaven," said Jesus, according to Mt 19:12. Matthew's gospel has coupled this statement with another of Jesus' sayings, about divorce. Exegetically, everything indicates that originally the statement had another *Sitz im Leben*. The text does not speak of the unmarried (*agamoi*), but of the unmarriageable, those not suited for marriage: "eunuchs," a word that had an undesirable sound in Jewish ears as well as Greek. It indicated an unsuitability for procreation and the founding of a family, which was in itself an abomination to the Jews. That scripture uses this particular word betrays the original context of the statement. Pharisees and scribes never stopped criticising Jesus and his disciples for all those ways in which they distinguished themselves from the other Jews (not keeping the Sabbath, eating with sinners, not fasting, etc.). If they denounced Jesus as a "glutton and a drunkard" (Mt 11:19), then it is evident that they might have ironically denounced as eunuchs the close companions of Jesus, who had left everything to follow him. Jesus took advantage of this situation: So you call my followers eunuchs! So they are—because they are under the spell of the kingdom of God that has been inaugurated with my coming. Not everyone can yield to its attraction, but only a few to whom God has given the special grace to discover the full overpowering hidden wealth and worth of the kingdom of God (Mk 4:11). Since it is God who has chosen them, all criticism must be silent.[2]

This original *Sitz im Leben* of the statement, still evident

[2] See a penetrating exegetical study in an evangelical journal: J. Blinzler, "Eeisin eunouchoi. Zur Auslegung von Mt 19:12," in *Zeitsch. f. Neutest. Wissenschaft* 48 (1957), 254–270.

from the use of the unpleasant-sounding word "eunuch," which had clearly been used in a polemic context, presupposes the *fact* of the celibacy of Jesus' apostles: there are those who "for the sake of the kingdom of God are incapable of founding a family." Jesus points out that his disciples who have discovered the hidden riches of the kingdom of God could not existentially do other than "leave everything" (*eunouchia*, incapacity for marriage) and "follow him." The gift of the coming kingdom held them so in its spell that they left everything joyfully and without counting the cost; it was not even possible now for them to go back to their married lives (Lk 14:26; 18:29). They could no longer devote themselves to goods and possessions (Mk 10:21; Mt 19:21; Lk 18:22). They could no longer concern themselves with their own livelihood (Mk 8:34; Mt 16:24; Lk 9:23). It was a matter of existentially not being able to do otherwise; in this sense they are truly "eunuchs." There are such people, says Jesus. Clearly this applies to the apostles. Jesus doesn't say that all are doing this, nor that they have to do it. Defensively and approvingly he establishes the fact: "*eisin eunouchoi.*" In any case, in the group of the disciples of Jesus there are those who have experienced this as a sovereign demand of God's inviting grace: "we have left everything and followed you" (Mt 19:27). For them it was the inner logic of their enthusiastic discovery of the kingdom of God: "for the sake of the kingdom of heaven."

In the synoptics the original experiential fact of this "inner logic" is already formulated as a demand. Whoever

wants to be Jesus' disciple must leave everything: "house
or brothers or sisters or mother or father or children or
lands" (Mk 10:29–30; Mt 19:29); that is, the old patriarchal
family group with its property and goods. Luke leaves out
"or lands," but adds "or wife" (18:29), apparently in connection with another passage (Lk 14:25–26).

We need not consider this interpolation as a doctrinal
qualification. As with all the Semites, "my house" to
the Jews stood for "all my possessions," and it was for the
Jews that Matthew and Mark were writing. Therefore the
expression meant "my wife" in the first place.[3] Luke, on
the contrary, was writing for Christians converted from
among the heathen, for whom this implication might well
have been lacking, so he had to add "or wife" explicitly for
his readers to grasp the content of Jesus' statement. All three
synoptics speak restrainedly yet positively about "leaving
one's wife" for the sake of the kingdom of God. But in
Luke the formulation of the demand has become less strict.
The term "leave" (in itself open to several nuances of
meaning) is weakened to "hate"—weakened, because for a
Semite "hate" in such a context meant "to love less."

Thus the meaning is to love God above everything. The
suggestion that whoever belongs to Jesus' group in a special
way cannot do other than leave everything and give up
married life is an authentic biblical fact, in its essence inde-
pendent of ancient ideas about man and the world. It can
only be explained on the basis of the incalculable inner

[3] See "Frau in Judentum" in *Jüdisches Lexicon* 2, Berlin 1928, 774; also
Oikia, in *Theol. Wörterb. z. N.T.* 5, Stuttgart 1954, 135, n. 9.

logic of a total surrender to the kingdom of God, next to which everything else pales by comparison. In the synoptic gospels, "celibacy" is not presented as an abstract ideal, nor as a requirement imposed from without, nor even as a desideratum. Jesus approvingly states a fact of religious psychology: in view of their joy on finding the "hidden pearl" (Mk 4:11), some people cannot do other than live unmarried. This religious experience itself makes them unmarriageable, actually incapable of marriage; their heart is where their treasure is. Paul already thematises this experience; he sees its inner logic as an ideal towards which all Christians are invited (1 Cor 7:7–8; 28–35).

Even Tertullian can be cited as a witness that innumerable clerics have remained unmarried for the Lord's sake.[4] In this statement one can see the lasting nature of this concrete religious experience in the life of the church, which Jesus had already spoken of in terms of *eunouchia*. Scripture knows no juridically binding connection between office in the church and celibacy, but it recognises something more fundamental—that the religious experience of the overpowering might of the grace of God's kingdom becomes for some people a condition which makes entrance into marriage impossible. The inviolability of this fact of religious experience has been upheld by the church in the east as well as the west. The law of celibacy in the western church is, with all its advantages and disadvantages, only a juridical formulation of the inner logic of a particular religious experience.

----

[4] "De exhort. cast.," 13, *Patrologia Latina* (PL) 2, 930.

TOWARDS A JURIDICAL EXPRESSION OF THIS EXPERIENCE: THE LAW OF CELIBACY

The Initial Conflict: Christianity and Married Life

Specific church legislation regarding clerical celibacy was not forthcoming for some centuries, for there were misconceptions in the evaluation of religious celibacy. In the first centuries of the church religious celibacy or continence was not only a Christian ideal but also a continuing inducement to heterodox tendencies.[5] Already in the Church of Ephesus, dualistic, pre-Gnostic trends were coming to the fore, against which the Pastoral Epistles protested: "These people would forbid marriage and the use of particular foods."[6] Later such theories would give rise to a schismatic church with its own hierarchy. Encratism (*enkrateia* means abstinence) is the collective name for these rigoristic tendencies and also the proper name of a sect founded in Syria or Mesopotamia and brought from there into the west. Epiphanius epitomised its spirit: woman is entirely a creation of the devil, man only half-way; above the waist he is a creature of God, but the rest of him was wrought by the devil. The union of both in marriage is thus doubly a work of the devil.[7] Already active in the second century,

[5] There is an extensive body of literature on this subject. See, for example, E. Schillebeeckx, *Marriage, Human Reality and Saving Mystery*, Sheed and Ward, New York 1966, vol. 2.

[6] See 1 Tim 4: 1–5, especially verse 3.

[7] *Adv. Haereses*, lib. 1, *panarion* 45, n. 2, in *Patrologia Graeca* (PG) 41, 833 (4).

this tendency was to increase until it became a massive threat to an authentic Christian view of life.

All the church fathers, even the rigorist Jerome, forcefully opposed all forms of Encratism or other attitudes inimical to marriage. Nevertheless many Christians had difficulty at first in reconciling baptism and being married —a feeling that had its origin in heterodox environments in particular but also prevailed among many Christians. It was not the one-sided emphasis on continence as such that was considered heretical, but the corollary notion that only those who practised complete continence comprised the true church of Christ, an assertion which ultimately implied the establishment of a schismatic church. The church itself therefore continued to defend the truly Christian character of married life on the basis of her understanding of herself as *Church*. This does not do away with the fact that during the first centuries the church placed true Christian perfection in *enkrateia* or continence. The tension in the early church between the ideal of chastity and the heterodox exclusivism of Enkratism can be seen as the struggle to give marriage as well as chastity a legitimate place within the church. The overemphasis on celibacy, or at least on continence, can be found among the unorthodox as well as among the orthodox (especially in Syria and Mesopotamia). The dividing line became clear only when in the patristic church the connection between Christian *baptism* and continence was considered to be essential.

Originally, then, the main problem was therefore not the relationship between office in the church and celibacy, but between *baptism* and celibacy. In the Syrian churches this problem lasted for a long time. As late as the third century, chastity was called "the crown of baptism" and was practised at such.[8] But this tendency probably had found an early foothold in the ancient church. The so-called second letter of Clement states that only the "pure in body" may share in Christ's body, the church; and that the kingdom of God shall come to pass when all fleshly lusts and distinctions of sex shall have disappeared.[9]

The apostolic fathers too had to warn against those who were inimical toward "women, wine, and the eating of meat,"[10] the three prohibitions of Enkratism. About 170 (when for the first time there was the threat of a schism—Tatianus was condemned in 172), Dionysius, bishop of Knossos, reproached a fellow-bishop in an area that was nevertheless orthodox for "requiring the heavy yoke of virginity to be laid upon the faithful," and he urged other bishops to be less strict in matters relating to marriage.[11] Also, the "letters of Ignatius" asked Polycarp, bishop of Smyrna, not to demand celibacy of his Christians.[12] In many apocryphal writings—not indeed recognised by the church as part of its literature, but widely read as devotional books in the fourth and fifth centuries—"continence"

---

[8] A. Vööbus, *Celibacy. A Requirement for Admission to Baptism in the Early Syrian Church*, Stockholm 1951.

[9] *2 Clem.* 14, 3–5; 12, 2 and 5.

[10] Funk, *Patres Apostolici*, v. 2, 174–175.

[11] Eusebius *Hist. Eccl.* IV, 23, 6–7; in PG 20, 286–388 (ed. Sourc. chrét., 31, pp. 203–204).

[12] *Ad Polycarpum:* PG 96, 245 (Texte u. Untersuch. 16, p. 80).

was overemphasized, though for the most part not in the sense of the schismatics. The idea expressed here was that for a married person who continues to have conjugal relations, salvation is out of the question. More dangerous— and yet perhaps more generally read than the apocrypha[13] —was a small book written toward the end of the second century by a Christian named Sextus, who drew from neo-Pythagorean sources and spread the Hellenistic notions that prayer and sexual intercourse are contradictory, and therefore even castration is to be recommended for the sake of contemplation.[14] Later this was literally applied by Egyptian monks and even by Origen.

Again in the third and fourth centuries, Enkratic tendencies became prominent. But now they caused the great church fathers of the fourth century not only to begin a deeper theological consideration of religious celibacy but also to defend more emphatically the goodness of the married state. On the other hand, it cannot be denied that a patristic exposition of marriage more often supported the Christian advantages of complete continence than it presented a reflection on marriage in itself. Time and again one finds the statement that marriage is good, but celibacy is better. A fundamental contempt for marriage is foreign to all the orthodox Christian writers, even those like Tertullian

---

[13] "Read by most Christians," said Origen (*Contra Celsum*, 8, 30: *PG* 11, 1559).

[14] Published in Cambridge 1959 and edited by H. Chadwick, the aphorisms of Sextus being for the most part translated into Latin by Rufinus.

or Jerome who go off on a tangent (in this respect rather exceptional among the patristic writers); but the biblical affirmation of celibacy often results in a disparagement of marriage among the fathers. All things considered, marriage was looked upon as a state of life for those who were "weaker": a kind of second-rate Christianity, although one repeatedly finds the warning not to look down upon married Christians as though one were already in a state of blessedness. In that time it was not the existence of celibacy or continence that had to be defended (that was evident for a Christian then), but the lawfulness of marriage for Christians. This climate of opinion can best be formulated as follows: marriage, a good gift of the Creator—although tainted in its sexuality by original sin—is intended for those Christians who cannot practise continence. This is expressed, among other things, in the patristic shift of meaning of the biblical idea of "bride of Christ." In the Bible, the church is the bride of Christ. By the very fact of his baptism, every member is incorporated into this bridal relationship, which—from about the time of Origen on—is extended to each individual believer. But gradually this idea was restricted to the "consecrated virgins," and in the fourth century this shift is an accomplished fact. So the person unmarried for the sake of God was thought to be the typical Christian, a view that was formulated in such a way as to cast a shadow upon the full Christian significance of the married state. Marriage—at least when it involved sexual intercourse, for the fathers also recognised continence in marriage—was thus often looked upon as a decent outlet for weaker Christians.

Against such a background it is understandable that along with the biblical motivation of celibacy "for the sake of the kingdom of God" there were sometimes questionable subsidiary motives indicating an anti-sexual feeling. Priesthood and marriage did not go together, for holiness and marital sexuality were mutually irreconcilable.[15] To make the ideal of celibacy still more attractive, family life was usually portrayed in an unfavourable light. Moreover, this had been a literary theme in the pagan world, exalting "free love" over life lived in the restraints of marriage. So pregnancy, birth, and the rearing of children brought only pain and hardship,[16] married life consisted only of tribulation,[17] it was described as an "unbearable bond" and a "heavy burden,"[18] a "drama full of woe";[19] people spoke of the "bitter joy of having children."[20] Among statements taken out of context from contemporary preaching or profane literature, we could compile almost the same notions—literary satire on marriage and family life can be found in all ages—which shows that such a collection of its nature

[15] St. Jerome, *Adv. Jovinianum* I, 34; *PL* 23, 256–258; Ambrose, *De officiis ministrorum*, I. 50: *PL* 16, 98; Innocent I, *Epist. ad Victricium*, c. 10: *PL* 56, 523; *Epist. ad Exsuperium*, c. 1: *PL* 56, 501; Siricius, *Epist. ad episc. Africae: PL* 56, 728, etc.

[16] Ambrose, *De Virginibus* I, c. 6, n. 25–26: *PL* 16, 195–196; Basil, *Epist.* II, 2: *PG* 32, 224–225.

[17] Jerome, *Adv. Jovinianum* I, 28: *PL* 23, 249–250; *Adv. Helvidium* 22: *PL* 23, 206.

[18] Ambrose, *De viduis,* c. 13, n. 81: *PL* 16, 259.

[19] Gregory of Nyssa, *De virginitate* 3: *PG* 46, 325–336 (cf. with pagan literature: P. De Labriolle, *Les satires de Juvénal. Etude et analyse,* Paris [n.d.], 192–197).

[20] Tertullian, *Ad. uxorem* I, 5: *PL* I, 1282–1283.

presents a distorted picture of people's real thoughts and feelings. A collection that is just as indicative in another direction can be made of passages full of praise and admiration for marriage and family life, also drawn from the same patristic literature (such collections indeed exist). The more satirical type serves an apologetic intent (to be sure, not praiseworthy), to make celibacy or continence attractive.

On the other hand, one should not overlook these negative aspects. Catholic historians do show a tendency in this direction. But it seems to me that in this way an injustice is done to the true greatness of the church fathers. People forget that the fathers' positive achievements on the subject of the evaluation of Christian marriage are the result of their hard struggle against the dualistic attitude of their times that was also an essential part of their own feelings about the world, and their own spontaneous reactions. When the positive contribution of the church fathers is presented as self-explanatory, then the whole significance of their hard-won victory over the ancient dualism is minimised, or the fathers are reproached for the wounds dealt to Christianity in the hard struggle against all forms of Enkratism and disapproval of marriage.

The local Council of Gangral, in which the Enkratism of Eustathius was condemned, provides evidence of one of the severest crises in the middle of the fourth century, especially in Asia Minor. In a balanced manner, this synod accepted the traditional Christian evaluation of continence and lifelong virginity but reacted against "the innovations which are in conflict with the gospel." From this condemnation we can learn something about the excesses of the time. Marriage was wholly rejected—married people were shunned like the victims of a plague and it was thought that they had no chance of salvation. The faithful refused to join with married persons in prayer. They were averse to receiving the sacraments from married priests (still common in those days) and in fact would not even attend their eucharistic celebrations. Women left their husbands, or dressed as men, or even deserted their children as a sign of their flight from the world. The bishops of Asia Minor reacted in a vigorous and level-headed way against such distortions of religious celibacy.[21]

Fundamental Viewpoints Shared by Both the Eastern and Western Churches

With this historical background, it is understandable that the first Council of Nicaea refused to make celibacy obligatory for church officials, in spite of the insistence of some members;[22] otherwise, the council was afraid it might feed the latent Enkratic tendencies. However, we know from documents of the fourth and fifth centuries that the celibacy of these church officials was highly esteemed.[23] Epiphanius, an otherwise vigorous fighter against all forms of opposition to marriage, even called celibacy the "ec-

[21] Mansi, v. 2, 1095ff.

[22] Socrates, *Hist. Eccl.* I, 11: *PG* 67, 101–104; Sozomen, *Hist. Eccl.* I, 23: *PG* 67, 925.

[23] Eusebius, *Demonstr. Evang.* I, 9: *PG* 22, 81; Cyril (of Jerusalem), *Catech.* XII, 25: *PG* 33, 757; *Nymesius, Epist.* 105: *PG* 66, 1485.

clesiastical law of the priesthood,"[24] thus concretising in spirit the so-called canonical rule of the Pastoral Epistles. His phrase *prepon estin* is noteworthy; celibacy is not a strict requirement but a sovereign ideal suggested by the very nature of the priesthood, an inner invitation given in ordination. In the same sense Eusebius of Cesarea says it is fitting (*prosèkei*) that those consecrated (*hierômenoi*) should have no further relationships with women.[25] Methodius, too, who wrote sublimely in praise of virginity, nevertheless opposed an obligation of celibacy for all.[26]

So the Council of Nicaea did not require the strict observance of celibacy; nevertheless it forbade marriage *after* receiving higher orders "according to an ancient tradition of the church."[27] We will return shortly to the meaning of this prohibition. At this point we should note too that this council also opposed all forms of opposition to marriage and refused to permit those who had allowed themselves to be castrated for reasons of Enkratism to be ordained. The rule that was clearly formulated for the first time by this general council—no marriage *after* the reception of an important office in the church—has remained fundamental in both the eastern and the western churches. Even the Second Vatican Council has remained true to it, in its Dogmatic Constitution on the Church, in spite of the wishes of some prelates who, contrary to the whole tradition,

[24] *Adv. Haer.* ii, panarion 48, n. 9: *PG* 41, 867, 868; see also panarion 59, n. 4: *PG* 41, 1021–1025, and *Expositio fidei* 21: *PG* 42, 823–826.

[25] *Demonstratio evang.* i, 9: *GCS* xxiii, 43–44.

[26] *Symposion*, Oratio iii, 13: *PG* 18, 82 (ed. *Sourc. Chrét.* 95, p. 121).

[27] Mansi, v. 2, 670.

wanted to make an exception for the diaconate. However, the concrete working out of this universal principle has proceeded differently in the east and in the west.

Canonical Legislation in the East

From the fourth century on, the eastern church began to choose its bishops almost exclusively from monks, who had already vowed themselves to celibacy. Towards the end of the fourth century, St. Synesius, who was appointed bishop after his marriage, had to stress that he accepted his appointment only on condition that he might continue marital relations with his wife.[28] Especially in Egypt and surrounding territories the celibacy of bishops had apparently become the custom. Yet from histories of the early church we gather that in the fifth century the situation was quite varied. Some priests and bishops were married; in Thessaly, the custom prevailed that those who were already married could keep their wives when they received their higher ordination, but that they must live as brother and sister; if not, they were deposed. The same rule was followed in Macedonia and Greece.[29] In 420 an imperial law decreed this for all the bishops.[30] In the sixth century Emperor Justinian decreed that a man who had children could not become a bishop and that a married cleric who became a bishop must treat his wife as a sister.[31] Here for the first

[28] *Epist.* 105: *PG* 66, 1485.
[29] Socrates, *Hist. Eccl.* v, 22: *PG* 67, 637.
[30] *Codex Theod.* XVI, 2, 44.
[31] *Codex Justin.* XLII, 1.

time—though without explicit reference to it—the "inheritance question" comes to the fore: one who has *children* (not just one who is married) may not become a bishop; "church" possessions may not be divided among the children. Note that a "Christian monarch" made this decision. In later legislation of the *Novellae* it was decreed that a bishop should be either unmarried or separated from his wife.[32]

It was only in the seventh century that the east decided to proclaim a definitive law at the synod of Trullo (692), giving universal legal force to a custom which had arisen more or less spontaneously.[33] The bishop was obliged to live in continence; if he had been married before his ordination, then he had to separate from his wife (who went into a monastery); however, he was still obliged to give her maintenance and financial support (in the first eleven centuries this was a strongly felt obligation). Priests, deacons, and subdeacons were not allowed to marry after their ordination; but if they had already been married, they might stay with their wives and have normal sexual relations.

Rome has never disapproved this eastern law, although in the past its approval has not always been very warm,[34]

[32] *Novellae,* VI and CXXIII.

[33] C. 6, 12–13 and 48; Mansi, v. 11, 944–948 and 965. Thanks to the *Decretum Gratiani* (d. 31, c. 13: ed. Friedberg, I, 114), the eastern legislation was also known in the Latin Middle Ages, along with the criticism made by the eastern synod upon the radical law of celibacy in the west.

[34] See *Decretum Gratiani,* d. 31, c. 14 (Stephanus IX, in 1058); III, tit.

even though the regulations of the synod of Trullo were really meant also as a protest against the western view. In the east, it should be noted, the same *ideal* of celibacy for clerics prevailed as in the west; but the eastern church considered exceptions to it as prompted and required by particular needs, especially pastoral ones.[35]

The Trullan regulations still apply in principle. But since the seventeenth century, marriage *after* ordination has also been *tolerated* for subdeacons, and now here and there this applies even to deacons and priests. Since the seventh or eighth centuries, bishops have been chosen from the ranks of monks only, a practice which still prevails in the whole present-day eastern church. The eastern churches united with Rome follow the Trullan law in principle; only a few local churches have simply taken over the Latin legislation.[36]

The Law in the West; Ordination as an Obstacle to Valid Marriage

In the west the development has proceeded somewhat differently. The first effort to sanction the increasing spon-

---

2, c. 6 (Innocent III); see Pius XI, *Ad catholici sacerdoti fastidium,* in *Acta Apostolicae Sedis (AAS)* 28 (1936), 24 and 28. The Second Vatican Council even praised these married priests (Decree on the Life and Ministry of Priests, c. 3, n. 16).

[35] See Epiphanius, *Adv. Haer.* 59, 4: *PG* 41, 1024. That was also the attitude of the eastern bishops at the Second Vatican Council.

[36] See J. Dauvillier, C. de Clercq, *Le mariage en droit canonique oriental,* Paris 1936.

taneous custom and to make celibacy, or complete continence for those who were married, into law for the higher clergy, can already be found in the west at the beginning of the fourth century at the (generally rather rigorist) synod of Elvira,[37] which involved a large portion of the Spanish clergy.

The first papal directives which were part of the same trend came from Pope Siricius, in 385 and 386, for priests and levites (deacons).[38] Although the synod of Rome, to which he refers, speaks of a "counsel" (*suademus*), it appears from his letters to Himerius and the African bishops that the pope is thinking of making it a requirement, an attitude which possibly has a connection with the ferment around Vigilantius. For it was just at this time that Vigilantius had caused a crisis in Rome on the issue of celibacy by his criticism of virginity, even of the Mother of God. The consequence of this was, according to Augustine, that "even many cloistered nuns, whose virginity was above all suspicion, decided to marry."[39] Perhaps the chronological juxtaposition of these two events—the church's condemnation of the current tendency and the first papal documents urging celibacy for the most important officials of the church (both acts of Siricius) signifies an inner connection between them. Historically, the *law* of celibacy

[37] Concilium Illyricum (*circa* 305–306), c. 33: Mansi, v. 2, 11 (see Denz., n. 52b and c).

[38] *Epist. decretalis ad Himerium* 7: PL 56, 558–559 (Denz., n. 89), and *Epist. ad episcopos Africae*: PL 56, 728.

[39] *Retract.* II, 22: PL 32, 639.

would then be partly the result of an actual crisis concerning celibacy that happened at the same time, one which deeply affected everything around it. In any case, the chronological combination is certainly suggestive.

The decisions of the Roman synod were also promulgated to Spain and Africa, where the same restrictions were enforced by local synods.[40]

Jerome confirms that in Rome and Egypt only virgins became clerics; or if they had been married before ordination, they abandoned common married life.[41] Because Pope Siricius had heard that priests (or bishops) were still producing children years after their ordination, he forbade (in his letter to Himerius) the practice of the cleric and his wife living together as brother and sister which, until this time, the church had accepted without question. For it had become evident, owing to the children, that continence in such marriages had not been more than a pious desire. A few years later Pope Innocent I expressed the same views in a dispatch to the bishop of Rouen,[42] whereby Gaul was placed under the law, so that here too local councils began to enforce the legislation regarding celibacy.[43] The synod of Orange (441) and of Arles (524) demanded a sort of

---

[40] Council of Carthage (390), c. 2:Mansi, v. 3, 692.

[41] *Contra Vigilantium*, c. 2: PL 22, 356.

[42] *Epist. ad Victricium* (anno 404), c. 10: PL 56, 523–524; and *Epist. ad Exsuperium* (bishop of Toulouse, A.D. 405), c. 1: PL 56, 501–502.

[43] Council of Orange, c. 22–24; Mansi, v. 7, 879; Council of Arles: Mansi, v. 7, 886. The aforementioned synodal interventions (before the ninth century) were compiled by Burchard of Worms in his *Decretum*, II, 108–118: PL 140, 645–646.

promise of perpetual virginity even before ordination to the diaconate. From considerations of humanity and justice (is it right for a priest who was married before simply to send his wife away upon his ordination?) Leo I (440–461) renewed permission for the priest who had been married before ordination to stay with his wife afterwards, but urged them to live in continence and in a "spiritual union";[44] on the other hand, he extended the obligation of continence to subdeacons.[45] Under Pelagius I (556–561) the "inheritance question" came up again, or more properly the *feudum presbyterale*, on the basis of which the sons of priests could inherit church property. When this pope ordained someone who had a wife and children to be a bishop, he added a clause to the notice of appointment providing that the children might not inherit any of the church's goods.[46] However, in all of this there was really no question of a law of celibacy, but only of a law of continence; the actual celibacy law dates only from the twelfth century.

In the period of the Merovingians, measures were taken to prevent the humane permission of Gregory the Great and Pope Leo (to live as brother and sister) from resulting in the actual invalidation of the law prescribing continence. Even the use of a common dormitory for clerics, or the practice of clerics living with the bishop, stems from this time. The *Ordo Romanus XXXVI* includes, along with the

[44] *Epist.* 167, *ad Rusticum* 3: PL 54, 1204.
[45] *Epist. ad Anastasium* 14, c. 4: PL 54, 672–673.
[46] *Epist. Pelagii papae Cethego patricio*: PL 79, 414.

ordination of priests and deacons, a liturgical blessing for
the wives they might possibly have, which indicates that
they too are to be dedicated to continence.[47]

Furthermore, the Merovingian synod had to keep on
stressing the law requiring continence,[48] for various reasons.
Even Jerome had said that he knew hundreds of bishops
who sympathised with Vigilantius' criticism of celibacy.[49]
On tombstone inscriptions of married bishops and clerics
piquant protests against celibacy were often found.[50] But
there was a more obvious reason, especially after Pope
Leo I. Already in the fourth century, the need of the priest
for a *single* life had been pointed out,[51] but now Pope Leo,
with generous confidence, had given permission to married
priests and deacons to live with their wives as brothers and
sisters after their ordination. This confidence in people
was somewhat too great; the practice of continence remained for the most part a dead letter until the eleventh
or even the twelfth century. While the eastern churches
maintained that there should be either no marriage (and
then no form of living together), or marriage and living

---

[47] N. 27; see M. Andrieu, *Les Ordines Romani du haut moyen âge*,
v. 4, Louvain 1956, 200.

[48] See *Monum. Germ. Hist.*, conc. aevi Merov., 125, 158, and 181:
councils of Tours (567), Auxerre (between 573 and 603), Orléans (541)
and Mâcon (583).

[49] *Epist.* 69, *ad Oceanum* 2: PL 22, 654; *Adv. Vigilantium*, n. 2: PL
23, 340–342.

[50] See *Dict. Archéol. Chrét. Lit.* v. 2, col. 2822–2827, and v. 10, col.
1973–1975.

[51] Ps.-Cyprian (prob. Pope Lucius 1 or Celestius), *De singularitate
clericorum: PL* 4, 835–870.

together, but with the full consequences of a real married
life, the Latin church until the twelfth century allowed its
clerics to be married, but required them to practise complete continence. Because of this psychologically abnormal
situation, the law of continence remained, as we have said,
a dead letter during these centuries. The reform of St.
Boniface and the Carolingian renaissance could not provide
any lasting remedy,[52] especially because all kinds of unfit
candidates had been ordained for political reasons. Through
the activity of Boniface, a "law of celibacy" had indeed
prevailed for a while in the ninth century, but from the end
of the ninth to the beginning of the eleventh century, there
was chaos once again, with all the accompanying consequences.[53] Simony in particular brought unworthy men into
the priestly office; the church became the victim of the
feudal system.

In 1023, Pope Benedict VIII preached his outspoken
sermons against the clergy who lived in concubinage or
were married.[54] The contemporary literature about this
situation is alarming. Peter Damian paints a sombre picture

[52] See the complaints of St. Boniface to Pope Zacharias: *Epist. 50 ad
Zachariam: Monum. Germ. Hist.*, epist. III, 299–302. The Frankish priests
claimed they had got a "dispensation" from Rome. Zacharias answered
that he had never heard of such a dispensation (ibid. 302–305).

[53] For the moral and political situation, see X. H. Arquillière, *St.
Gregoire VII*, Paris 1934; A. Fliche, *La réforme grégorienne* (Spic. Sacr.
Lovan., 6), v. 1, Louvain-Paris 1924, and A. Dumas, *Les vices du clergé
et les aspirations à une réforme de l'Eglise séculière*, in A. Fliche and
V. Martin, *Histoire de l'Eglise*, v. 7, Paris 1943, 476ff.

[54] *Monum. Germ. Hist.*, Const. Imperatorum, v. 1, 70; see Mansi, v.
19, 343ff. (i.e. the Council of Pavia under the same pope, which forced
all these priests to resign).

of the Italian clergy.[55] A bishop of Liège complained that if he should enforce the church's disciplinary rules, he would have to dismiss his entire clergy.[56] Many priests justified their conduct by saying that for them marriage was a social necessity.[57] The councils of Limoges and Bourges (1031) forbade anyone's being ordained to the subdiaconate unless he freely made a promise of complete continence or left his wife.[58] At a Synod of Rome (1059), Pope Nicholas II told the faithful not to attend the Masses of priests who had wives nor receive the sacraments from them.[59] This was a counterpart of the earlier synod of Gangra. Out of zeal to rise above the moral chaos, this "iron age" neglected all humane feelings, which earlier popes and councils had taken into consideration. Decrees attempting to improve the hopeless situation began to accumulate.

In the long run the struggle seemed so fruitless that some bishops gave it up and advised their priests, "Si non caste, tamen caute," i.e., if you cannot leave your wife—in fact, such a marriage remained still valid then—at least be discreet about it.[60] In other words, don't flaunt your concubine—e.g. by walking arm-in-arm through the streets.[61] In local

---

[55] *Liber Gomorrhiae: PL* 145, 159-190; *Contra intemperantes clericos: PL* 145, 387-424; *De caelibatu sacerdotum: PL* 145, 379-388, and his *Opuscula: PL* 145, 124, and 410.

[56] Ratherius, *Itinerarium Romanum* 5: *PL* 136, 585-586.

[57] Atto of Vercelli, *Epist.* 9: *PL* 134, 117-118.

[58] Can. 6: Mansi, v. 19, 503 (laicised priests were in fact allowed to marry).

[59] Can. 3; Mansi, v. 19, 897-898.

[60] *Monum. Germ. Hist.* SS., v. 7, 346-347.

[61] See, for example, the Council of Pavia in 1018 (or 1023?): Mansi,

synods, bishops even expressed the idea that the law of
celibacy was an absurdity. Nevertheless, all the reform
synods in the eleventh century, from Leo IX to Urban II,
continued to insist on celibacy, and for the most part explicitly also upon the grounds of church tradition: "sacrorum canonum instituta renovantes."[62] In other words, the
farther the church progressed in history, the more the
church's tradition of celibacy became a canon, a norm and
a confirming motive.

The reaction against violations of the law of continence,
which had already begun during the tenth and eleventh
centuries, was definitely developed only with the reform
of Gregory VII, and finally Gregory won his case. This
Gregorian reform even became the starting-point of one of
the most exciting spiritual and mystical movements which
the west has known, and which in the twelfth century
purified the atmosphere to such an extent that the peaceful
theological speculations of the early scholastics became
possible. A somewhat radical means of resolving the crisis
over celibacy was the idea of simply proclaiming the marriage of (higher) clergy invalid. From the eleventh century
on, people began to reflect upon the concept of the *sacramentum*, including its application to marriage, and hence
clerics could appeal to the sacred character of marriage in

---

v. 19, 345–346. See H. Maisonneuve, "La morale d'après les conciles des
Xe et XIe siècles," in *Mél. Sc. Rel.* 18 (1961), 1–46.

[62] Synod of Mainz (1049): Mansi, v. 19, 749; of the Lateran (1059):
Mansi, v. 19, 907; under Gregory VII: in 1073 (Mansi, v. 20, 173), in
1074 (v. 20, 413–414), in 1078 (v. 20, 510); under Urban II: in 1089 at
Melfi (v. 20, 723), in 1095 at Clermont (v. 20, 906).

order to justify themselves in being married in the full sense of the word. The declaration of invalidity of clerical marriages removed their new hope.

The reaction to this—pro and con—was so strong that Gregory VII felt himself obliged to forbid every attempt to find a theological and historical basis for the marriage of priests.[63] Nowhere did he himself declare explicitly that the marriages of the higher clergy were invalid; however, he treated them as such. Even the First Lateran Council (1123) under Pope Callixtus II, stated only that such a bond must be broken (*disiungi*).[64] Not until the Second Lateran Council (1139), under Pope Alexander II, was the invalidity made into a law, in this sense: marriages of sub-deacons, deacons, or priests *after* their ordination were invalid—in other words, concubinage; candidates for the priesthood who were already married might not receive any higher orders unless they severed all relations with their wives.[65] Thus it is only since this council that the higher clergy in the west have been required to observe not only continence in marriage but strict celibacy. Since the council decision and its confirmation by Alexander III in 1180[66]

[63] *Monum. Germ. Hist.* SS., v. 5, 436, in connection with the anti-Gregorian writing of a Bishop Ulrich von Augsburg (*Monum. Germ. Hist.* libelli de lite, v. 1, 255).

[64] Mansi, v. 21, 286.

[65] Mansi, v. 21, 715. Pope Innocent II had announced four years earlier at a provincial synod of Pisa: "*sancimus* huiusmodi copulationem matrimonium non esse." The Second Council of the Lateran stated: *censemus*, "we judge, we are of the opinion," which sounds somewhat milder.

[66] *Decretales Greg.* IX, lib. IV, tit. 6, c. 1 and 2.

and Celestine II in 1198[67] the following rule holds for the Latin church: only those who freely accept "celibacy for the sake of the kingdom of God" are admitted to the higher offices in the church.

The so-called medieval "scholasticism of the secular clerks" expressed in the second part of the *Roman de la Rose* (around 1277, by Jean de Meung), nevertheless continued to oppose the law of celibacy "in the name of Nature."[68] In the thirteenth and fourteenth centuries, too, the reaction still found many adherents, especially canonists, and even bishops; they tried to get the eastern regulations adopted by the west. In the fourteenth and fifteenth centuries, the actual concubinage of priests again assumed larger proportions. False papal bulls purporting to allow marriage were often appealed to. But as far as the faithful were concerned, the idea of the priesthood was already essentially bound up with the single state. St. Brigitta protested strongly against a bishop who was said to have stated: "If I were pope, I would repeal the law of celibacy."[69] At the councils of Constance and Basle a petition was presented to allow secular priests to be married, as they were in the east;[70] but it did not succeed. At the Council of Trent, the

[67] *Decretum LIV: PL* 206, 1254.

[68] C. Paré, *Roman de la Rose,* Montreal 1947.

[69] *Revelationes* VII, c. 10, v. 2, Rome 1628, 202–203.

[70] *Acta Conc. Constanc.* ed. H. Finke, v. 2, 589, and *Conc. Basil.,* ed. J. Haller, et al., v. 8, 121. On the concubinage of priests in pre-Reformation times, see O. Vasella, "Über den Konkubinat des Klerus im Spätmittelalter," in *Mélanges Ch. Gilliard,* Paris 1944, 269ff. The bishops frequently tolerated concubinage because heavy financial penalties were

bishops recognised that the law of celibacy was not a positive divine law; some council fathers voiced the opinion that it would be better to repeal the celibacy law in order to calm down the feelings of the people. After much discussion, however, Trent confirmed the stand that the church had taken at the Second Lateran Council: if anyone says that clerics with higher orders (or religious with solemn vows) can enter into a valid marriage, let him be anathema.[71] It was not stated whether this decree was based upon a divine law; also, no position was taken on the question of whether clerical celibacy was just a church law or whether it implied a personal vow at the same time.

Even after the Tridentine decision, there were still bishops of unimpeachable integrity who strove to free secular priests from the law of celibacy. In Germany, the emperor Ferdinand and Maximilian II pleaded with the

exacted for it. The criticism of the Reformation was therefore reasonable; see O. Vasella, *Reform und Reformation in der Schweiz*, Münster 1958, 28.

[71] Sess. 24, can. 9 (Denz., n. 979) (see CIC, can. 132, no. 1 and can. 1072). This canon is only a reaction against the Reformation, which cast doubt upon the competence of church authority; it does not contain any dogmatic affirmation, e.g. that priesthood and marriage in essence exclude each other, and that therefore ordination makes marriage invalid. Trent is only defending the legitimacy of its practice in these rules, from after the Second Lateran Council. Since 1931 (*AAS* 23 [1931], 120v.) a *written* statement is required before the subdiaconate, in which the candidate asserts that he knowingly and willingly accepts celibacy freely, not being forced in any way to do so. Of course, such a statement can conceal a psychological conflict which has perhaps not yet become apparent.

pope to dispense the German secular clergy from this law. Pius IV seriously considered complying with this request, but remained under pressure from Philip II to put off his decision[72]—indefinitely, as history shows. The actual formation of seminaries for candidates for the priesthood in the seventeenth century made the law of celibacy into a generally accepted reality. In the eighteenth century, at the time of the Enlightenment, new attacks upon the celibacy of priests began, mostly from "outside," but many priests too breathed the spirit of the Age of Reason. The French Revolution officially removed priesthood as an impediment to marriage. In addition, under the attrition of all kinds of ideas connected with the revolution, the old order and the ideals of medieval Christendom dissolved. Gradually the situation of the Church and the world which we have today developed. Under these pressures the church became somewhat milder in giving dispensations to those leaving the priesthood, but maintained the principle itself more than ever. The desire to do away with the celibacy law continued to exist, and became concentrated most of all in France and South America.

In 1898 a false bull was circulated in which Leo XIII was said to have removed the law for Latin America. In Czechoslovakia, too, many priests claimed the right to marry.[73] In France, virulent literature against the celibacy of priests

[72] See G. Constant, *Concession à l'Allemagne de la communion sous les deux espèces par Pie IV*, Paris 1923, on celibacy, 546–612 and 1013–1023.

[73] See *AAS* 12 (1920), 585.

continued to appear after the Modernist crisis,[74] even on the Catholic side. The church reasserted the principle of celibacy repeatedly,[75] but meanwhile permission was given for various reasons for married men to become priests.[76]

In 1959 Fr. Spiazzi, a renowned Italian Dominican, cautiously published some objections to the celibacy law with an eye on the forthcoming Second Vatican Council.[77] His article became a sensation. Not long afterwards, Pope John XXIII made known (in an audience with the superior-general of the Sulpicians) that no relaxation of the celibacy law was to be expected.[78] Since then, many articles have appeared in various countries which cast doubt on the desirability of an automatic coupling of celibacy and priesthood, whether in view of ecumenical, psychological, or sociological considerations, or on account of the decrease in priestly vocations, or because the theological foundations of Christian celibacy are no longer valid, given our modern view of mankind and the world.[79] Seen against

[74] The book *Le mariage des prêtres*, Paris 1911, by Abbé J. Claraz, was especially well-known, and placed on the Index.

[75] *Mirari vos* of Gregory XVI (1832), *Qui pluribus* (1846) and the *Syllabus* (1864), prop. 74, of Pius IX; *Pascendi* (1907) of Pius X; *Ad catholici sacerdotii fastidium* of Pius XI; and *Sacra Virginitas* of Pius XII.

[76] See a dossier on this in *Inform. cath. intern.* of 1 Dec. 1963, 25-34.

[77] In *Monitor Ecclesiasticus* 84 (1959), 339 vv. (*Docum. cath. 57* [1960], 402-404).

[78] *Docum. cath.* 57 (1960), 847.

[79] Of interest here is the book of the Dominican prior of Marseilles, a loyal Catholic and a deeply committed priest, which was not passed by the censor. Because he was apostolically convinced of the significance of his plea on behalf of so many of his colleagues in the priesthood, he

the background of the church's past, the present "celibacy crisis" is obviously not a new or exceptional phenomenon. It is only one manifestation of a tendency which has been present throughout the history of the church, at times latent and at other times more pronounced, and which exists alongside another tendency which has been predominant since the days of the early church. Thus there is no reason for alarm. The problem is certainly real, and not in the least superficial. Is the doubt which has never disappeared during the whole course of the church's history a legitimate one which must be honoured as such? Are the arguments for a new course of action sound? The fact is that a desire can be right even if the arguments supporting it happen not to be sound and hence might block the new development. Therefore we should consider next the motives which have led to a law of celibacy.

gave up his position as prior, asked for permission to leave, and returned to the lay state. After that he published his book: P. Hermand, *Condition du prêtre. Mariage ou célibat?* Paris 1963. On the Dutch side, see, among others, an anonymous brochure, *Celibaats-crisis. Suggesties van een priester*. The Hague 1963; H. Brentjes, *Het celibaat*, in G-3, June 1963, 179–188; J. Fraats and M. Schlijper, "Het celibaat," in *De Nieuwe Linie*, 1 Feb. 1964; J. Brouwers, "Bezinning op het celibaat," in *Sanct. Euch.* 26 (1964), 90–94; R. J. Bunnik, "Het celibaat," in *Te Elfder Ure* 11 (1964), n. 7–8. See also Bernard Cardinal Alfrink, "Over het priesterlijk celibaat," in *Anal. v. het Aartsbisdom* 36 (1963), 166–181.

2

THE EXPLICIT MOTIVATION FOR CLERICAL CELIBACY IN THE HISTORY OF THE CHURCH

IN THE PATRISTIC WRITINGS
Motives for Religious Celibacy in General

Gradual Christianisation of already existing motives in pagan religions. We have seen that in the synoptic passage about the "eunuchs for the sake of the kingdom of God" celibacy was not specifically formulated. Jesus refers only to a special religious experience of the kingdom of God, which for some people puts marriage radically outside their view of what is possible for them. Subsequently, people began to reflect upon this experience. The spontaneous gesture of not marrying or of living in continence as an inward, unreasoned consequence of seeking the kingdom of God then became consciously motivated.

In all reflective thinking, ideas, assumptions, and judgements peculiar to their own time play an unmistakable role. Now it is a fact that in pre-Christian and pagan times "continence" and "religious observance" were linked together in certain instances, and that this connection was also up to a point explicitly motivated. Celibacy, or at least continence for certain periods, for religious reasons, is thus not specifically Christian. In many religions there is a certain connection between cultic observance and sexual abstinence; it is also found in Israel (see Ex 19:15; 1 Sam 21:5). The first Christians were therefore already confronted with reasoned motives for continence, even before they accepted the faith. Historically, the specifically Christian motives can be intelligible only against the background of these ancient reasons. An explicit consideration of Christian celibacy will almost unavoidably be influenced by them.

Some facts are known about the nature of these ancient motives. In a study of pagan religious attitudes toward continence, D. Fehrle has stressed that in the Greco-Roman world continence was urged for two reasons: anyone who enjoyed the special love of a god ought to forsake the love of a mortal creature (this is called the motive of intimacy or nearness to God); and sexual intercourse has something defiling about it which betokens the presence of evil spirits, so whoever stands at the altar must restrain himself from the sexual act (the "Vestal principle" or motive of cultic purity).[1]

In view of the Christian motivation of celibacy, these religious-cultural preconceptions appear to be important. The two basic motives seem to contain so many false

[1] *Die kultische Keuschheit im Altertum* (Religionsgesch. Vers. u. Vorarb. 6), Giessen 1910. These ideas were not typically Greek, but deeply influenced by eastern thought; see H. Jeanmaire, "Sexualité et mysticisme dans les anciennes sociétés helléniques," in *Mystique et Continence* (Etudes Carmelitaines), Paris-Bruges 1952, 51–60.

judgements that at first sight it may not be at once apparent whether or not authentic elements are also hidden there; yet the first Christians were living in a period when these ideas were widespread. From the standpoint of the historical Christ-event they began with difficulty to reinterpret these things. It seems certain to me that Paul, for whom the existential inability to enter into a conjugal life had been a spontaneous consequence of his discovery of the mystery of Christ, was influenced in his conscious reflections upon it by these two motives from religious antiquity, which were traditional for him. In 1 Cor 7:32–35 he speaks of a certain "division" and competition between the love of God and conjugal love; on the other hand in 1 Cor 7:5 he connects prayer (contact with the "good spirit," God) with continence. (In the ancient world sexuality is regarded as the sphere of "evil spirits," but this attitude Paul will purify.) Obviously the difference between the pagan and Christian attitudes toward continence is at first apparent not in the motivation—which is similar on both sides—but in the fact that for the heathen, continence is the result of human purpose or asceticism, whereas the Christian calls it a *charisma:* a pure gift from God (1 Cor 7:7; Mt 19:11). This biblical emphasis on grace continued throughout the early church, which therefore asked God's grace in common intercessory prayers "for all who are living in continence."[2] Characteristic for the early church was not the motivation in itself, but the inclusion of pagan preconceptions in a biblical view of grace. Thus it was possible that

[2] *Constit. Apost.* VIII, c. 10, n. 11, ed. Funk, 490.

in and through the Christian *practice* of celibacy, these
motives began eventually to be critically examined and
gradually purified, a process that has been going on now for
twenty centuries. We shall proceed to analyse the main
lines of its development.

In the early church, there was a conflict between the
Christian and the pagan ideals of celibacy—that is, between
celibacy as charisma and celibacy as an ascetic achievement.
The church fathers seldom mention celibacy without warning against self-willed pride in the ascetic achievement of
self-control, which was what celibacy was for the pagans.
Yet at times the ideal of continence as a gift of God also
went astray and degenerated into libertinism and quietism.
Therefore the church fathers began to take over the pagan
ascetical ideal, but (after various one-sided views had run
their course) seeing it in a true Christian perspective. The
Christian synthesis was succinctly summarised by Augustine: "Da quod iubes et iube quod vis." "Give me, God, the
ability to accomplish what you command me to do, and
then command whatever you will."[3] In other words, the
charisma must become viable *within* the human response
that follows upon it, and this in turn is also a gift of God.
The difference between the Christian and pagan ideals of
continence lies at the outset exclusively in the acknowledge-
ment of saving grace; the explicit motivation was of the
same nature.

During the course of church history, the "pagan" mo-

[3] *Confessiones* x, c. 29, 40; see also Jerome, *In Gal. Comm.*, 5, 22: *PL*
26, 449.

tives were continually coloured by this idea of grace, fundamentally anchored in Jesus' statement about the connection between the grace of the kingdom of God and continence—"to whom it is given" (Mt 19:12). The pagan religious and cultural motive of "nearness to God" was to be modified eschatologically by Paul into the motive of the coming parousia of the Lord (1 Cor 7:29). This eschatological motive re-echoes Luke's in "equal to angels" (20:35–36), in the "sons of the resurrection" (Lk 20:36), and in the fact that there will be no marriage in the final kingdom of God (Mt 22:30ff.). Most modern authors take the phrase "equals to angels" as simply meaning not having bodies. But this is a misconception. The synoptics and Christians until far into the Middle Ages did not look on angels as "pure spirits" simply in the sense of having no bodies, of lacking flesh and blood. For the men of ancient and biblical times, angels were mighty, concentrated personalities, Powers, who stood always in God's presence, prepared to do his bidding swiftly. That is what is suggested in the idea of the unmarried condition as being "equal to angels"—something very different indeed from our modern attenuated notion of sweet angelic natures for which a body is unsuitable or unnecessary; or if it is necessary, it will be only the desiccated physicality which this view associates with "celibacy." For the church father, a celibacy "equal to angels" called up the idea of force, the power and might of beings with a free, concentrated centre for their lives, ready for the service of God and men, like the angel who came to Tobias. *That* is what it is to live eschatologically: to be completely free and available in the service of God and one's fellow man—something that will reach its full development only through the resurrection of the flesh, when we shall be "sons of God, being sons of the Resurrection" (Lk 20:36).

"Having an inner intimacy with God"—this general religious motive became more prominent as the meaning of Christian celibacy when, later on, the immediate expectation of the parousia began to fade. This was not presented as an argument but stated as a generally known fact: continence brings one closer to God, as Athenagoras had simply stated it.[4] Prayer and continence evoke one another.

Going back to the original experience: Jesus and Mary. In the fourth century, people recognised that continence with its double motives is not only an ideal to strive for; it had already been concretely realised in two persons, Jesus Christ and Mary. Now these two were considered as the real foundation of religious virginity;[5] remember that it was only in the second half of the fourth century that Mary's virginity was recognised by practically everyone in the church. In this way the objective connection made in the Bible between religious celibacy and the kingdom of God was concretised. There is an inner connection between

[4] Athenagoras, *Suppl. pro christianis,* c. 33: PG 6, 965.

[5] "Christus virgo, virgo Maria, utrique sexui virginitatis dedicavere principia" (Jerome, *Epist. 48, ad Pammachium,* c. 21: PL 22, 510). See H. Koch, *Adhuc virgo, Mariens Jungfrauschaft und Ehe in der altkirchliche Ueberlieferung bis zum Ende des 4. Jahrhunderts,* Tübingen 1929, and *Virgo Eva, Virgo Maria. Neue Untersuchungen über die Lehre von der Jungfrauschaft und der Ehe Mariens in der ältesten Kirche,* Berlin 1937.

religious celibacy on the one hand and the fundamental figures of salvation on the other: Jesus and Mary, Jesus' mother, the type of the church. Thus the pagan motives, though not denied, were rediscovered in an absolutely new way from the viewpoint of the mystery of Jesus, at least in their explicit formulation, in which the pagan influence was yet apparent. Praise of virginity became to an ever greater extent the praise of the virgin Mary; she *is* virginity already embodied.[6] This concretising of the biblical relation between continence and the kingdom of God received its general formulation in the concept of "total consecration to the Lord."

Priesthood and Celibacy

The foregoing analysis concerned celibacy and continence in general. As far back as the third century, but particularly in the fourth, other accents came to the fore when continence and the priesthood were connected. The first decree making continence obligatory for the clergy, from the synod of Elvira, illustrates this. An explicit justification is not given, but canon 19 of the synod states that priests and bishops, on whom continence is henceforth to be imposed, may continue to live with their wives, and keep their familial and business relations and responsibilities; it was only required of them that they should not travel too much out of their own diocese on secular business. The motive of

[6] Gregory Nazianzen, *Poëma II*, "In laudem virginitatis": PG 37, 521–578.

complete availability for apostolic service thus played no part at all (and this was true until the twelfth century). It was only required that they "abstain from their wives" and "have no children." In other words, the motive is clear; the unsuitability of sexuality for someone who stands at the altar, that is, the ancient motive of "cultic purity"; the sacred and the "impure" are mutually exclusive. Also in the fourth century, this motive became more and more prominent in patristic literature, even as the only motive for continence in the clergy in contrast to that of monks, ascetics, virgins and widows.[7] This ancient pagan and Jewish motive was, however, transformed into a "Christian" one in the light of Adam's fall: sex is not degrading simply as such (anthropological dualism), but on account of the historic sinfulness of mankind (original sin). Man's inner being was disordered. For the clergy, then, the motive of intimacy with God is relevant. In contemporary literature, however, one usually finds the motive of "cultic purity": the priest, as (sacramental) offerer, ought also to be an offering in his own life; sacred service does not accord with the actual exercise of sexuality. The "suitability" of continence for priests which is mentioned by Basil and Eusebius of Cesaria (*prepon estin prosèkei*), specifically

[7] Origen, *Contra Celsum* VII, 48: *PG* 11, 1492; Ambrose, *De offic. min.* I, 50: *PL* 16, 98; Jerome, *In Tit. comm.* 1, 8–9: *PL* 26, 568–569; *Adv. Jovin.* I, 34: *PL* 23, 256–258; Pope Siricius, *Epist. ad Him.* 7: *PL* 56, 558–559; *Epist. ad episc. Africae*: *PL* 56, 728, and *Epist.* 10: *PL* 13, 1184; Augustine, *De coniug. adult.* II, 21: *PL* 40, 486; and later: Isidore (of Seville), *De eccl. off.* II, 10: *PL* 83, 790–791. It is noteworthy how all of these authors follow each other with almost the same words.

indicates the *unsuitability* of sexual life for the consecrated. Old Testament texts from Leviticus and 1 Sam 21:2–7 (the sacred in contrast to the impure), and Is 51:11 played an important role here, especially since Jerome (and others with him) had said: "omnis coitus immundus" (in each sexual encounter there is something impure), or as Minucius Felix had previously put it, "even lawful conjugal relations fill many of us with shame."[8] Many papal letters point out, and rightly so, that officiating at the eucharist requires chastity and freedom from concupiscence;[9] but then this becomes understood as complete abstinence from conjugal relations as well, as if there could be no "conjugal chastity." The ancient idea that cultic service required continence is still of great influence without being actually reflected upon. In the liturgical rite of ordination the exhortation, "imitamini quod tractatis"—a formulation which obviously breathes the spirit of Gregory I and his time—is elaborated as follows: you who celebrate the mystery of Christ's death must keep your body pure of immorality and concupiscence. This is self-evident, but here the meaning is that you must also keep yourself free from conjugal intercourse. The sexuality of married couples, good in itself, is

[8] Jerome, *Adv. Jovinianum* 1, 20: PL 23, 238; Minucius Felix, *Octavius* 31, 5: CSEL 11, 45. The opposition between *sacredness* and the *impurity* of sexuality is clearly apparent in Ambrose's *De officiis ministrorum* 1, 50: PL 60, 96–102.

[9] Siricius, *Epist. ad Him.* 7: PL 56, 558–559; and *Epist. ad Episc. Africae:* PL 56, 728: priests must live in chastity so that the Mass that they offer will be pleasing to God. Also Pope Innocent 1, *Epist. ad Exsup.* 1: PL 56, 501 and *Epist. ad Victr.* 10: PL 56, 523–524.

viewed in the light of celibacy and original sin, not only in its relativity and ambiguity, but even with a tinge of "coming close to unchastity," a notion which later sermons for the people were to elaborate still more strongly.[10]

Thus it is manifest that from the third century on, church leaders came to be looked upon in the light of the *Old Testament* priesthood and the high-priesthood of Christ, a parallel inspired by the Epistle to the Hebrews. In this way the apostolic and sub-apostolic "prophetic type" of church official developed into the "cultic type": the classical image of the priest, the one-sidedness of which was countered only by the Second Vatican Council in the Decree on the Ministry and Life of Priests. This cultic idea of the priesthood immediately called to mind the Old Testament and ancient idea of the priest, following the spirit of those times: the sacred service of the altar did not allow any sexuality. The biblical mystique of being "incapable of marriage because of the kingdom of God" remained as a spirituality for monks, ascetics, and virgins; the continence of priests was viewed rather in the line of "cultic purity."

Finally, sociological motives played a part too, though historically one should not give them so much weight. We have already noted that the children of married clergy could inherit church property, something that was not very welcome to popes and emperors. In the early Middle Ages this motive came to have greater weight, so that even the

[10] See, for example, Peter Damian, *De caelibatu sacerdotum*, 3: PL 145, 384.

possible children of priests were declared "unfree," lest
through inheritance the wealth of the church should be
wasted away.[11] If we bear in mind the sociological structure
of the medieval family,[12] we can more readily understand
that the church wanted to keep her freedom against the
power of the uncle (*avunculus*, especially the mother's
brother) of the priest's children (*nepotes*, hence nepotism),
who had his own way in feudal families. Celibacy was an
effective means to this end. It must be admitted that this
motive did play a part in the law of celibacy, but not to a
decisive extent, unless perhaps with one or another of the
popes of the Iron Ages. Even then the financial factor was
still not dominant, but rather the freedom of church authority, which wanted to neutralise the machinations of
family authority (the uncle). The medieval tendency towards papal absolutism certainly played a part in this, but
as far as I can determine, not directly in establishing the law
of clerical celibacy (or continence). Indeed, this had already been settled. Anyone who interprets the law of
celibacy as an ecclesiastical abuse of power for the benefit
of the hierarchical organisation, although this did occur in
certain areas, makes a caricature of history.

New motives did not appear after the patristic period.
A certain synthesis of the whole earlier tradition can be
found in the old liturgy of the veiling of virgins and the

[11] See the Council of Pavia, c. 3 and c. 4; Mansi, v. 19, 353. See W.
Plöchl, *Geschicte des Kirchenrechts*, v. 2, Vienna 1955, 163.

[12] See J. Le Goff, *La civilisation de l'Occident médiéval*, Paris 1964
("La famille," 349–354, esp. 354).

blessing of marriages.[13] Here the church's full assent to married life is expressed: it is a blessing from God which is not taken away either by original sin or the Flood. Thus marriage signifies more than it is in and from itself: it points to union between Christ and his church. But this *deepest* meaning can also be lived directly, in virginity. According to these sacramentaries, marriage and celibacy are two complementary manifestations of the same mystery of salvation: marriage expresses it in a veiled manner, religious celibacy in an eloquent sign. The origin of this celibacy is Jesus.

IN THE MIDDLE AGES
The Evangelical Movement in the Middle Ages

After celibacy had become law with the Gregorian reform, the pre-scholastics began to turn their attention to it. Many historians have not noticed that the most profound insights into clerical celibacy can perhaps be found in the twelfth century.[14] These early scholastics certainly saw the difficulty: how can the church, in view of Paul's statement "concerning the unmarried I have no command from the

[13] For a comparison of the consecration of virgins from the *Leonianum* (ed. Mohlberg, 1103–1104), with the bridal veiling of the *Gregorianum* (ed. Lietzmann, 110–112, nr. 200, 1–11), see E. Schillebeeckx. *Marriage, Human Reality and Saving Mystery*, v. 2, New York 1966, 306–307.

[14] The medievalist L. Hödl, "Die 'lex continentiae' Eine problemgeschichtliche Studie über den Zölibat," in *Zeitschr. f. kath. Theol.* 83 (1961), 325–343, is one of the few who have recognised the full significance of their thought.

Lord" (1 Cor 7:25)—make celibacy obligatory for the clergy? They saw clearly that the church's law of celibacy, and especially the refusal to recognise the marriage of priests as valid, implied a new existential experience of the priesthood. The eleventh and twelfth centuries constituted one of the most stirring evangelical periods in the history of the church, in which people often followed an oscillating course between "orthodoxy" and "heresy."[15] These ages came under the spell of the apostolic life as it was described in the gospels, particularly as a lay movement, although priests also joined in. Eventually this richly variegated spirit achieved a clearer form through the charismatic gifts of Francis and Dominic, the former more in the direction of the laity, the latter tending rather towards a new evangeli-cal inspiration of the priesthood in its care of souls. In this evangelical-apostolic movement, celibacy was seen as only one dimension of the total evangelical commitment. The "sacrament of orders" was therefore no longer considered as just an "office," but as at the same time essentially a basis for an evangelical spirituality. One could say that for the first time in church history the authentic biblical inspira-tion of celibacy "for the sake of the kingdom of God"— formerly an ideal only for monks, ascetics, virgins, and widows—was now connected with office in the church and transcended, at least in principle, the ancient motive of "cultic purity."

[15] See especially H. Grundmann, *Religiöse Bewegungen im Mittelalter*, Hildesheim 1961, and E. Werner, *Pauperes Christi: Studien zu religiösen Bewegungen im Zeitalter des Reformpapsttums*, Leipzig 1956.

The New View of the Canonists

It was not theologians but canonists who first became aware
of this new spirit of the times. The synodal sermon of the
canonist Ivo of Chartres gives a model exposition of the
new view of the priest's state of life.[16] "Poverty"—that is,
self-denial—and self-effacement (*humilitas*) became along
with celibacy the existential characteristics of the new idea
of the priest.[17] Like the evangelical ideals of poverty and
humility, celibacy too is the expressive exponent of the
apostolic situation of the priest, whose interests are not
centered in things secular, but "in the things of the Lord,"
the concerns of the kingdom of God. "*Sacer ordo*," holy
orders, was henceforth the name of the higher offices in the
church, not on account of their higher official function or
"spiritual power"—as would be claimed later—but on
account of their existential commitment to a state of life
—namely, celibacy.[18]

In other words, to be a priest included celibacy, not
because of the function as such but in its concrete-
existential being. The Gregorian reform had borne fruit:

[16] *Sermones* II, "Sermo synodalis de excellentia sacrorum ordinum":
PL 162, 513–519. Here we find the "classic image of a priest" (and the
"type" of all the major and minor orders).

[17] Loc. cit., col. 513 and Epist. 34 and 37: *PL* 162, 46 and 49–50.

[18] "Non dicuntur *sacri* ordines propter effectum quem habent in
suscipientibus sed *propter statum suscipientium*, scilicet inferiores a
subdiaconatu et infra tenentur *ad continentiam*" (Stephen Langton,
Summa quaestionum, cited by Hödl, loc. cit., 339; see also Guido of
Orchelles, *Tract. de Sacramentis*, c. 8, n. 189).

no longer was it a matter of a *law* of celibacy, but of an enthusiastic *desire* and a freely accepted spirituality of the priesthood. The canonists, always concerned about precision, also found a new formulation for this situation: the *ordo*, that is, the sacrament of orders itself, contained within itself a *votum continentiae*. The canonical law of celibacy became interiorised: there is an inner connection between priesthood and celibacy. Therefore the church, on the grounds of her power of the keys, can impose celibacy on her office-holders. The *law* of celibacy was founded on a *vow* of continence, inherent in the sacrament of orders.[19]

Although this view goes somewhat too far, its basic idea seems to us to be that of the gospel itself: there is an inner affinity between the evangelical "office in the church" and the equally evangelical "celibacy for the sake of the kingdom of God." On the grounds of the ecclesiastical refusal to consider the marriage of those already ordained as valid, the people of the twelfth century spoke of an *indissoluble* bond; in this they went too far. This view nevertheless rests on a very humane regulation. Centuries earlier, Gregory the Great had not wanted to cause trouble for those already married by making them leave their wives upon ordination, if they had not made any promise in this regard beforehand: "That is improper and hard," he said.[20] To prevent this damage to human relationships the pope decreed that henceforth no one was to be ordained subdeacon who had

[19] This idea is to be found first in the writings of the canonist Gratian: *Decretum*, d. 28: ed. Friedberg, I, 100.

[20] *Epist. 44, ad subdiaconum Petrum* I: PL 77, 505–506.

not made a promise of continence beforehand in full freedom, in order to prevent what had happened before one came under the law of celibacy (i.e., a valid and legitimate marriage) being broken up in an inhuman manner. The biblical idea of a freely accepted charisma was thus viewed as a *presupposition* of the personal call to the priesthood. Thence came the principle of the idea that the law of celibacy presupposed a free commitment to a state of life to begin with. As early as the seventh century, the Fourth Council of Toledo (633) spoke of a "professio castitatis," a promise of virginity, which must be made in the presence of a bishop before one received higher orders.[21] It was precisely this solemn "profession to live in virginity"—in other words, this constitutive pledged word—that the canonists considered to be an impediment to the validity of a marriage, not the ordination itself, abstractly viewed as the reception of an office in the church. Even though this "profession" was in their opinion inwardly *required* by ordination, the canon lawyers could nevertheless so integrate it into their notions of the monastic solemn vow that it became an impediment to a valid marriage.[22] This new view was established thanks to the great canonist Roland Bandinelli, later Pope Alexander III, who laid the foundations for the present canonical view of marriage in the Latin church. The sacrament of orders, he said, is an

21 Gratian, *Decretum*, d. 28: ed. Friedberg, I, 101.

22 See L. Ott, *Untersuchungen zur Theol. Briefliteratur der Frühscholastik* (Beitr. z. Gesch. Phil. Theol. Mitt., n. 34), Münster 1937; on the doctrine of "vows" in the twelfth century, see 303-313.

"annexum voto solemni,"[23] i.e., ordination is not only an objective invitation to receive the charisma of celibacy (as we shall state in our synthesis), but in essence it is already (at least implicitly) a "promise of continence."[24] Thus celibacy becomes a part, not of the abstract concept of "ecclesiastical office" but rather of the evangelical "concretely existential" understanding of it. The casuistical proposition that whoever freely accepts ecclesiastical office with this vow attached to it is *ipso facto* also obliged to celibacy must be called consistent with the canonical principle. Observe carefully that the fundamental idea is not that the church chooses her ministers only from among those faithful who, charismatically inspired, have chosen celibacy (that would make it into a principle of selection); but instead celibacy is an obligation that goes with the commitment to a state of life of a minister of the church. This is the new insight that still permeates all the present legislation in western canon law. Peter Lombard "sanctioned" this view for the Middle Ages: not ordination, abstractly and formally considered as such, but the "solemn vow" implied therein is an impediment to a valid marriage.[25] That is why celibacy before ordination is a non-obligatory "evangelical counsel"; but after (and with) ordination it is an ecclesiastical obligation (though freely accepted).

---

[23] Edited by M. Gietl, *Die Sentenzen Rolands nachmals Papstes Alexander III*, Freiburg 1891, 273.

[24] Roland, *Summa:* ed. F. Thaner (*Die Summa Magistri Rolandi*), Innsbruck 1874, 117.

[25] *IV Sent.*, d. 38, c. 2: Quaracchi edition, v. 2, 967.

Qualifications Made by Theologians in the
New Image of the Priest Forming the Basis of the
Subsequent Traditional View

The theologians remained rather reserved in their attitude
towards the discovery with which the canonists were so
happy, and they had good reason for it. Alexander of Hales
saw the difficulty. How can the church "impose" a spontaneous and free promise? Alexander replied: the church
forces no one into continence, but joins ordination with
celibacy, and that is her right; anyone remains free to
choose whether or not to aspire to ecclesiastical office (with
this implication). If a man chooses this office freely, then he
obliges *himself* to celibacy.[26] But this solution still did not
satisfy the theologians. They were aware (via the *Decretum
Gratiani*) that in the eastern church, ordination *per se* did
not include a solemn vow of celibacy. They preferred to
make a qualification—and this is an essential supplement to
the opinion of the canonists: the connection is an interior
one; office in the church invites the recipient to celibacy.
But actually the obligatory union between the two is only
imposed in the Latin church by the power of the keys. In
contrast to the canonists, the theologians stated their position matter-of-factly as follows: there is in fact a church
law of celibacy, for concretely the decisive factor is not
the vow, but the *law*. Luckily they did not abandon this
idea but continued emphatically to maintain their opinion
that however much religious celibacy factually is funda-

[26] *Glossa in IV Sent.*, d. 24, n. 7, ed. Quaracchi, 417.

mental to the "essence" of the sacrament of orders, formally speaking the power of enforcing it rests entirely and exclusively in the church's power of the keys. This theological insight unavoidably implies that the inward connection between church office and celibacy is most meaningful, but not compelling, not *essential;* in other words, there is only an inward affinity between the two, though it is a very close one. The disadvantage of this theological insight is, however, that the question is thus shifted onto the level of conceptual thematising, and takes no account of the original experience of the "existential inability to be otherwise," whereby the so-called "inward affinity" becomes indeed a sovereign demand for the individual concerned. The medieval theologians had thus not grasped the whole problem.

In our study of clerical celibacy we are indebted to the insight of the canonists as well as to the critical reserve of the theologians. Together they transmit two facts to us through their original thinking: somewhere there must be an *inward* relationship between the evangelically lived "ecclesiastical office" and "celibacy for the sake of the kingdom of God" (canonist trend), but conceptually and reflectively one cannot speak of an *inwardly compelling* relation (theological trend). The binding forcefulness of that relation is only dependent on the canonical law which, in their view, is of great value for the church but not necessary—to this one would, of course, have to add that the deepest foundation is the evangelical experience of "personal inability to do otherwise" overlooked by the medieval theologians. In the dialectic of these two points of view, seen in the light of scripture and tradition, we touch the two poles of the real problem. The inner relationship between evangelical office and evangelical celibacy is also stressed by what the eastern as well as the western church sees as the ideal apostolic norm: *after ordination* (sacramental investing with office) one *may* not marry. The western church has enforced this practice of the universal church to the extent that ordination has been made into an impediment to a valid marriage: after ordination one *cannot* marry—unless with an ecclesiastical dispensation which simultaneously forbids any further exercise of office.

Given the actual legislation of the western church, we can conclude that the medieval viewpoint in any event rightly points out that ultimately one comes up against the personal desire of the candidate to obligate *himself*. The church does not oblige anyone to become a priest. But on the basis of her mission to interpret the scripture, she has the right—the power of the keys—to impose restrictions in the light of scripture on the manner of life of those who are, after all, *her* ministers. On the basis of the biblical connection between religious celibacy and the kingdom of God, she has concretised the state of life of all who wish freely to accept office in the church into a Christian way of life that makes them, because of an intimate love of God, available to all in a special way, without a binding relationship to one person. Therefore she permits only those who feel themselves called to the venture of celibacy to enter the ranks of her official diaconate. So we can see that in this medieval view, biblical celibacy for church officials is at the same time an apostolic counsel, a church law and a personal life commitment, freely accepted with God's grace, in the service of the *corpus eucharisticum* (Christian purification of the cultic continence common to all religions) and of the *corpus mysticum* (Christian transposition of another general religious motive for celibacy, freedom from an exclusive form of human companionship, marriage, so as to be at the service of mankind). Christ and, subordinate to him, his mother are the living examples of this Christian manner of life.

However much it may have been obscured by human failings or too-worldly church politics, this has remained the heart of the ideal of clerical celibacy down to the present day. That the church has been living for eight centuries now in the light of this insight speaks well in any case for the religious and theological grandeur of the twelfth and thirteenth centuries, perhaps less well for the originality in thinking of these later ages. Yet the fact that opposition has also continued down to our present day, questioning whether ordination includes (at least implicitly) a vow of celibacy, indicates that although medieval theology has made a great contribution to the theory of celibacy, it has nevertheless struck somewhere an as yet unsolved difficulty. Has theology done too little justice to that biblical *experience* of "existential inability to do otherwise" (*eunouchia*)?

From this positive theological analysis it should have become evident (though only in a few broad outlines) that a so-called speculative theology which does not try to think creatively precisely *in* intelligent rereading of history is liable to be left hanging in the air; and that on the other hand a theology which restricts itself to an evaluation of present-day existence without relating it to the historical dimension of the *past* will not only utter haphazard, stupid things about that past (to the extent that it is mentioned at all) but will at the same time rashly overlook an authentic and existential dimension of our *present-day existence* as well. Then we find ourselves in a phenomenology that denies itself, because it simply by-passes one essential dimension of human existence, and thereby inevitably warps in advance the dimension that is most important and most fascinating to us—the future.

II »
A Critical
Reflection and
Attempted
Reappraisal

3

CELIBACY FOR THE SAKE OF THE KINGDOM OF GOD

OUTMODED ELEMENTS IN THE TRADITIONAL MOTIVATION

The questioning of religious celibacy is fostered in our own day not only by the new idea of man, but also by the new insight that has been affected by it and stimulated by the Second Vatican Council: the idea that *all* Christians are called to the perfection of holiness and to apostolic zeal for the kingdom of God in the church and in the world. This new insight, crystallised at the Council in the Dogmatic Constitution on the Church, showed clearly that theology in the past had not spoken carefully enough or in a sufficiently qualified manner about the superior value of Christian celibacy. In their arguments about it the theologians had insufficiently taken into account that it is the vocation of every baptised member of the church to love God undividedly with heart and soul and with all his strength. Thus married life was reduced to a second-rate kind of Christian life. At the same time, precisely because of this reduction, what is *really proper* to religious celibacy was not presented unequivocally and in its specifically Christian essence, at least in the explicit reflections on the subject. It is apparent from the idea that has been approved even on the conciliar level that the problem is more difficult and more involved than we had been given to understand from church history and theology, or at least from what was reflectively expressed therein. The fact that the Dogmatic Constitution *Lumen Gentium* emphatically refused to reserve the "undividedness" of heart to those who accept eschatological celibacy calls for consideration. The working draft of the text still showed the old view: "undivided love" and "consecration to God alone" were seen as characteristic of religious celibacy. Purposely, however, the non-Christian, ultimately Roman and Greek elements (i.e., the competitive opposition between love of God and love of man) were scrapped in the definitive text. This text reads: "This [virginity or the celibate state] is a precious gift of divine grace given by the Father to certain souls, whereby they may devote themselves *the more easily* to God alone with undivided heart."[1] Total consecration to God and undivided love for him are required of *all* Christians without exception; according to this conciliar text, celibacy gives only a certain "facility" in making this general mandate truly real.[2] The insertion of the words

[1] C. 5, n. 42 [in *The Sixteen Documents of Vatican II*, NCWC translation, Boston: St. Paul Editions]. Since a distinction is made here in the "undivided love" of Paul, 1 Cor 7:32–34 is cited only in a relative sense. Therefore the text itself does not say "1 Cor." but "cf. 1 Cor." In the technical jargon of the council, this always means that the biblical citation is not to be taken *per se* in its precise biblical meaning and context; in other words, in this case it implies a certain distance from the literal *expression* of Paul.

[2] How difficult it is to set aside the old point of view is apparent even

"more easily" speaks volumes for the new approach.

Also, "striving for perfection," as it is called in Catholic tradition, can no longer be identified with the religious life of celibacy, poverty, and obedience. Nor can we consider this characteristic as reserved for monks and nuns and as such denied to married Christians in the world; for that too has been resolutely rejected by the Second Vatican Council. The call to holiness, to boundless perfection like that of "your Father in heaven," is—as a gift of God—addressed to all men, not only to those who remain unmarried for the sake of the kingdom. Whoever designates "striving for perfection" as the vocation proper to one who desires to live a Christian life in religious celibacy actually misses the calling of all men to holiness.[3]

---

from translations of this conciliar text, whereby the non-Christian element is once more smuggled in. Thus one reads in the French edition of *Osservatore Romano* (18 Dec. 1964): "pour que plus facilement *et* d'un cœur sans partage ils se consacrent uniquement à Dieu dans la virginité ou dans le célibat." The unjustified insertion of "et" radically alters the conciliar text. This translation harks back to a former *working-* text, of which just this point was emphatically corrected for the final version. The former text read: "chastity consecrated to God . . . is a sign whereby a person dedicates himself totally to God." (*Schema const. Dogm. de Ecclesia,* Vatican City 1964, "textus prior, non emendatus.") Against this idea it was rightly pointed out that baptism itself is such a sign for all Christians. [Translator's note: The English reader will observe that the English NCWC translation falls into the same error observed in the above French version: "*due to* an undivided heart" also seems to imply that this undividedness belongs only to the celibate state, not to all Christians. Cf. the Latin text: "Inter quae eminet pretiosum gratiae divinae donum, quod a Patre quibusdam datur (cf. Matt. 19:11; 1 Cor. 7:7), ut in virginitate vel coelibatu facilius indiviso corde (cf. 1 Cor. 7:32–34) Deo soli se devoveant" (*AAS* LVII, 30 Jan. 1965, 48).]

[3] See the Dogmatic Constitution *Lumen Gentium* (c. 5, n. 40).

The statement that the reason anyone accepts religious celibacy is that he "desires to follow Christ *more perfectly*," or wants to belong to God *completely*, is likewise unacceptable, since it discriminates against Christian married people who by virtue of their baptism are just as fully consecrated to God *in all thing*, with heart, soul, and body. Anyone who denies this is still clinging to the idea that the married life of Christians is a second-rate Christianity. Even the term "exclusive" love for God is ambiguous, for to love God above all things can never mean for a Christian that love for fellow man is excluded or depreciated. For loving God never means that one neglects others in order to love God alone and not one's fellow man. Certainly in all things God is the ultimate aim, but this is the law of the gospel for every married Christian too.

But it might be objected that *this* way of loving God— in chastity—is an evangelical *counsel*, transcending the general obligation. This objection overlooks the fact that this counsel—from the Sermon on the Mount—is not setting forth the characteristics of some Christians but the essential requirements of being Christian at all. St. Thomas Aquinas expressed this lucidly.[4] Love knows no bounds.

---

[4] "Praeceptum dilectionis Dei, quod est ultimus finis christianae vitae, nullis terminis coarctatur ut possit dici quod tanta dilectio Dei cadat sub praecepto, maior autem dilectio limites praecepti excedens sub consilio cadat. Sed unicuique *praecipitur* ut Deum *diligat quantum potest*, quod ex ipsa forma praecepti apparet, cum dicitur: Diliges Dominum Deum tuum ex toto cordo tuo": *C. pestif. doctr. retrah. hom. a relig. ingr.*, c. 6 (*Opuscula Theol.* Marietti edition, Turin-Rome 1954, ii, n. 759), 165.

Of course, what the command to love—without limits—includes for me here and now is revealed to me by the particular situation that confronts me; in this way every Christian will be shown from time to time how his love measures up to "loving as Christ loves." But this standard of Christianity is for everyone: the Sermon on the Mount applies to each person in his own state of life.

Vatican II speaks of celibacy as the "easier means" of realising the general Christian undividedness of heart. This, too, is a traditional idea; many spiritual authors speak of celibacy as "the safer and easier way"; celibacy frees one "from those obstacles which might draw him away from the fervour of charity and the perfection of divine worship."[5] But this idea must also be handled with great care. The council is speaking within the perspective of the new concept of man and does not mean to imply any depreciation of secular values. Tradition spoke of "being free from worldly cares," but the council sees the Christian care for the things of the world in the perspective of the kingdom of God as one of the fundamental tasks of the layman in the world. Marriage with its cares (in the sense of *concerned involvement* with mankind and the world) is not only a good secular value but a Christian value too. Being a married Christian in and with the world is a positive Christian vocation: married people are not sanctifying themselves *in spite of* their marriage.

Naturally this state of life has its own dangers and threats, but these can be overcome with God's grace on

[5] Dogmatic Constitution, *Lumen Gentium*, c. 6, n. 44.

the basis of its sacramentality. This is just what makes it worth while to take upon oneself the difficulties involved in the realisation of this deeply human and Christian value, marriage; it is a sign of confidence in God and moral-religious courage when people find it worth while to realise its deeply human and Christian value, in spite of all the difficulties connected with it. By not marrying man indeed frees himself from the difficulties which are part of the married state, but on the other hand he finds himself psychologically in a state of life which brings other and sometimes greater difficulties along with it. The unmarried person who is not integrated psychologically, emotionally, and morally is the best example of this. The "easier and safer way" of celibacy is thus unmistakably to be taken in a very relative sense, and therefore it cannot *as such* be considered as having any absolute superiority over married life.

One could perhaps still say that by not exercising even humanly integrated sexual activity one can hold in check the tendency toward a humanly unworthy exercise of it, so that for the truly integrated man, the dangers peculiar to sexuality are lessened. In a certain limited respect celibacy places the integrated man—or rather, one who is on the way to such an integration—in a more favourable position. Married sexual life is of a kind that—for the benefit of the marriage itself—certainly involves man wholly; and because our human condition is tainted by sinfulness, and the humanising of sexuality is a not-yet-fulfilled endeavour, this central human activity can find

an ally in human concupiscence and egoism by which the
good gift of marriage can be somewhat spoiled. Perhaps the
integrated celibate avoids this danger, and in that sense the
unmarried person reserves all his attention for God and his
fellow man. But still all of this is only a *relative* way of looking at it. Not for nothing does Paul say that whoever is by
nature "sexually over-endowed"[6] does better not to live
in abstinence, but to marry. The actual assistance that the
married person has in the humanising of his sexuality because (and insofar as) he is fascinated by the human and
Christian *values* of marriage as his personal vocation is
missed by the celibate in his effort to integrate his sexuality
(for he has it too) in a human and Christian way, since he
has renounced the positive realisation of the values of
marriage. For him the integration of his sexuality has to
come from another source, from the love of God and other
forms of spending himself for his fellow man. If the person
who remains unmarried for religious motives is not strongly
under the influence of these values, his vocation to celibacy
threatens to go awry, from the very nature of his situation;
and his celibacy as well as his task of integrating his physical
nature with all its own tendencies becomes a failure.

Thus the "safer and easier way" still remains very ambivalent as a motive for celibacy, in spite of certain advantages—which are not *automatically* given, but come
about only in and through one's *actually entering into* the
religious values for the sake of which the celibate has

---

[6] That is the actual meaning of *hyperakmos:* 1 Cor. 7:36. Trans.: com-
pare the RSV: "If his passions are strong. . . ."

renounced the secular values. Each of the states of life has its own advantages and difficulties, and at the same time misses the advantages which are to be found in the other state. Further on, we will see how this relative motivation can become part of a deeper foundation, and then how it can take on another meaning.

The pagan, Greco-Roman motive of the "undivided heart" for God is in any case not to be maintained as the basic foundation for the meaning of Christian celibacy, at least not when people put such an "undivided love for God" over against love for man and the values of married love, as though they were competitive.

STEPS TOWARDS A MEANINGFUL MOTIVATION FOR OUR OWN TIMES
General Phenomenology of Celibacy on the Grounds of a Special Experience of Secular Values

Celibacy cannot be made religiously meaningful if its value as a *secular reality* is not first clarified. Something which is not clear in its own mundane reality can hardly function as a *sign* that makes another, supernatural reality more easily understood or more attractive. Some of the new theological interpretations have mised a good opportunity by overlooking this in their sign theory. This short-circuit also explains the tendency to call celibacy (as a value) purely and specifically Christian, which is contradicted by historical facts. Consequently a phenomenology should first be presented of celibacy as a plan of life, because one wants to devote oneself entirely to social work, art, science, the physical welfare of mankind, or the social, political, and economic improvement of life on the national, international, or global level. The realisation of noble secular human values for the sake of their own worth can obviously contain within it an *invitation* to place oneself entirely at the service of these values, passing up other, deeply valuable possibilities for one's life, namely marriage, so as to put oneself entirely at the disposal of the realisation of these values.

The positive choice of the single life thus always stands upon a double value-basis. On the one side, in marriage one individual (rightly) lays claim to the loving care and complete devotion of the partner to such an extent that the marriage relation would suffer if one of the partners took upon himself such an all-consuming job that there was danger of his placing his partner in the background in order to do justice to his own life's work. In this sense the meaningfulness of celibacy is derived from the high value of marriage. On the other side, just on account of their intense appreciation of human values, some people find that it is a concrete necessity in their lives—a vocation—to put themselves wholly and entirely at the call of a particular value. It is possible and meaningful that a person, having realised the proper nature of both values which are at stake, together with an intense desire to realise his life commitment, might decide voluntarily to live a single life. In this case, besides respect for the human conjugal relationship, the individual's choice of celibacy also implies that the decision to refrain from sexual activity, provided that it is psychologically and emotionally integrated, will be *inwardly suited* to promoting this special dedication to the chosen value. In that sense voluntary celibacy for the more intense realisation of a value is really a freeing of love (towards that value) and an elimination of difficulties which could block that particular realisation.

Thus purified of incorrect reflective argumentation this traditional motive, which was also adopted by the council as a justification for celibacy, is phenomenologically sound. The analysis of human experience shows that celibacy can be a condition of *special* total availability accompanying the specialised and concentrated activity for the realisation of some great value for mankind. Our new conception of the world and man does not detract from this. Hence it is surprising that people today should be so upset when this deeply human phenomenon likewise turns up among the faithful who want to devote themselves in a concentrated and specialised way to a *religious* value. In this case, does our new appreciation of secular reality suddenly make meaningless this primeval human capacity for being entirely caught up by *value?* Cannot religious values necessitate the same sacrifice as the devotion to other noble values on a human level?

Celibacy, then, for the sake of the realisation of a human *value* is most meaningful (although never a compelling necessity in itself), and a generally recognised fact among mankind; for certain individuals it can even be an urgent vocation. ("Here I stand. I cannot do otherwise.") To ascribe this intuition of mankind to a particular conception of man and the world clearly is a form of rationalism, not even meaningful from a humanistic point of view. To put it another way, phenomenologically the voluntary choice of celibacy for the sake of the realisation of a value is the expression of a special sensitivity for something of deep importance in human life which merits this total consecration. Its realisation can therefore become one's primary aim, an aim which justifies the sacrifice of other values. Only if the appreciation of religious values diminishes can religious celibacy become a fundamental difficulty even *theoretically*. (I do not refer here to the possibility that someone, perhaps justifiably, may conclude that he has made a mistake in his own vocation.) Phenomenologically, celibacy evokes the idea of a "concerned commitment": the awareness that a certain realisation of values is a matter of urgency for humanity.

Not only the attraction which the value has for the person himself, but also his consciousness of responsibility for his fellow man supports his celibacy. Authentic celibacy is the opposite of celibate egocentricity. Therefore it cannot be said that the function in this case replaces marriage; instead there is a compelling experience of a value which excludes other very meaningful possibilities for a particular person in a concrete instance. The actual deprivation of marriage can only be made up for through renewed relationships with one's fellow man, and ultimately with God.

Remaining Single as the Implication of a Special
Religious Value-Experience: "For My
Sake and for the Gospel"

The same phenomenology holds for the religious celibate:
the church has also understood it in this light in her living
experience of celibacy before her explicit reflection on its
Christian meaning. In the atmosphere of total readiness for
sacrifice and service in order to realise a value which is
worth giving up for other valuable things, the religious
celibate must seek for a renewed self-expression and "motivation." First, of course, we should make it clear that,
phenomenologically, such a way of life essentially implies
the need to recognise other human and Christian ways of
living as well—of Christians, that is, who do marry. For
mankind and the Church as a totality, marriage is a necessary vocation. The realisation of *total* value thus presupposes the *complementary nature* of married and single life.
From this point of view the tendency of the past to look
upon marriage as a second-rate kind of Christian life was
markedly unchristian from the very beginning; the pagan,
Greco-Roman motivation of celibacy was still at work
there. But on the other hand, the victory over this pagan
notion leaves the fundamental affirmation—the meaningfulness of celibacy—untouched. Married life belongs to
another kind of value-realisation that is also Christian and
human. The phenomenology of celibacy thus also means
that being single in itself, taken purely as a fact, has no
higher value than being married. To be single is in itself of

no value, unless it arises from the sovereign demands of some other value. (This can also have meaning for someone who wanted to marry but through force of circumstances did not find the right man or woman, even though such a case is different, too, because it is not a matter of vocational choice. It is not simply the fact of being single that is of value but rather a meaningful commitment to this role in a new realisation of values.)

Scripture speaks of celibacy "for the sake of the kingdom of heaven" (Mt 19:12) and in order to care for "the affairs of the Lord" (1 Cor 7:32): "for my sake and for the gospel" (Mk 10:29). The value towards which this celibacy is directed is the concrete *Person* of Christ and his life work: the establishment of the kingdom of God. Celibacy thus means a personal adherence to Christ and to his life's work: "both" are so absolutely worth while that they inspire some—"those to whom it is given"[7]—towards a specific life commitment for which they give up the value of marriage. Therefore we can speak of a mystical or contemplative (personalist) motive ("for my sake") and of an

---

[7] "Not all men can receive this precept (*touton logon*), but only those to whom it is given . . . He who is able to receive this, let him receive it" (Matt. 19:11-12 [RSV]). The ordinary translation of the Greek *choorein* by "receive," in the sense of understand, is increasingly doubted by exegetes. It means rather "to give space to, make room for," "to take into oneself," "to cope with, tackle, be equal to." In any case, the parallel Aramaic and Hebrew words for *choorein* never mean "to understand something intellectually." *Touton logon*, literally "that word," on account of its Semitic background (*dabar*) can mean a thing, a matter (here, continence itself) as well as a word. Thus, "Not everyone can do it . . . Let him who can accomplish it, do it."

apostolic motive ("and for the gospel"), so essentially and inwardly bound together that the two form but one total motive. The personal adherence to Christ and apostolic service are indeed essential characteristics of the Christian life in general. But the fact that some people give up other values for it (marriage in particular) indicates that they want to realise this value—the central element of the kingdom—in a *special way*. Here an entirely different sensitivity to value is present. So the new Dogmatic Constitution on the Church states: "The evangelical counsels which lead to charity join their followers to the church and its mystery in a special way."[8] Thus there is no question of a monopoly, but of a special manner whereby a distinctive form is given to the one single universal call to evangelical holiness and the apostolate. Joining this to the traditional elements (which we have treated above), the Dogmatic Constitution formulates this "distinctive quality" and "specificity" as follows:

This state of life . . . is a more direct imitation and a perpetual representation in the church of the form of life which the Son of God accepted in entering this world to do the will of the Father and which he proposed to the disciples who followed him. This state of life . . . clearly *manifests in a very special way* that the kingdom of God and its needs are raised above all earthly considerations.[9]

[8] *Lumen Gentium*, c. 6, n. 44. The phrase "in a special way" is repeated in chapters 5 and 6, precisely in order to exclude any monopoly of holiness and apostolate.

[9] Loc. cit., c. 6, n. 44. [Translator's note: Again I had to retranslate

"A more direct imitation (*pressius imitari*)" of Christ clearly alludes to the biblical "following of Christ." Strictly speaking, there is only one evangelical counsel in the gospel (i.e., remaining unmarriageable for the sake of the kingdom of God, Mt 19:10–12) about which no divine command has been given, according to Paul's explicit statement: "Now concerning the unmarried, I have no command of the Lord" (1 Cor 7:25). One who does not follow this counsel can certainly attain "perfection in love," whereas all the other evangelical counsels are indispensable for all Christians in order that they might realise in actual fact the universal vocation contained in the perfection of love. For all Christians, both the commandments and the evangelical counsels are necessary for perfection in love. Only celibacy for the sake of the kingdom of God is an evangelical counsel which does not have to be practised in order that this perfection in love may be attained; therefore Christian celibacy is the only evangelical counsel properly so called and is left entirely up to the will of the individual Christian. Indeed, it is the evangelical source and centre of what will later develop into the "religious life."

---

the Latin text. The NCWC translation is noticeably different from the Dutch version. Cf. the Latin text: "Formam quoque vitae, quam Filius Dei accepit, mundum ingressus ut faceret voluntatem Patris, quamque discipulis Ipsum sequentibus proposuit, idem status pressius imitatur atque in Ecclesia perpetue repraesentat. Regni Dei denique super omnia terrestria elevationem eiusque summas necessitudines peculiari modo patefacit; supereminentem quoque magnitudinem virtutis Christi regnantis atque infinitam Spiritus Sancti potentiam, in Ecclesia mirabiliter operantem, cunctis hominibus demonstrat" (*AAS*, loc. cit., 51).]

The gospel sees living in celibacy as one (possible) *Christian* way of life, meaningful in Christian terms on the authority of the gospel. The personal choice to live one's life according to this possibility can be traced back to having been moved by the gospel, specifically insofar as it proclaims the Christian significance of this state. The fact that an individual happens to be moved by the gospel in this particular manner—i.e., that the religious motive appeals to him in such a way that from then on he wants to plan his life according to it and give it a concrete embodiment—is naturally based on a personal sensitivity, which is a reflection of God's spirit working toward salvation in him. In this sense it is a very personal vocation and a response to the saving action of God, who has caused him to experience these religious motives so strongly. Seen from this angle, God stands at the origin of Christian celibacy.

But we would fundamentally misunderstand celibacy as a possible way of Christian life guaranteed by the gospel if we were to think of it as a *choice* made possible by revelation between a "natural good" (marriage) and a "supernatural good" (in this supposition: remaining unmarried). Celibacy, like marriage, is one possibility for any human life. Both can be lived in a meaningful *Christian manner*. In this sense, married people as well as celibates can live "with an eye on the kingdom of God." But the important thing is to determine what is the *directly* specifying value that a person has in mind when he undertakes celibacy as a way of life. Celibacy for the sake of other secular values (science, art, social work, etc.) is directly specified by these values, which are not primarily religious, although a believer might also live a celibate life in a Christian way for the sake of one of these other values—a social-political career, for example —thereby giving it a religious dimension. But that is not what people mean when they speak of celibacy for the sake of the kingdom of God. Because there is a danger that we might mistakenly think of this latter religious celibacy as a sort of choice between God and the secular value of marriage, we ought to try to determine the proper nature of Christian celibacy more exactly.

Directing one's life exclusively to God, or consecrating oneself to him exclusively, is an intention that of itself has no concrete content; hence in doing this one runs the danger of pursuing a phantom. Even Thomas Aquinas pointed out that all our ideas about God stem from our experience with the things of this world and with salvation history.[10] In our new existential experience, this point has become clearer. Man himself, along with the concrete world in which he lives, including the whole sweep of its history, is the only locus for truth. If God speaks, it is through mankind with his whole world and all its history; only this reality can convey the voice of God's revelation. This is the reason why there is no contradiction between the word of God that reaches us through the statements of scripture and that which comes to us by way of our present existential experience; scripture gives us the norm, showing how we can distinguish God's word faithfully in the demands of our here-and-now existence.

10 *Summa Theol.* i, q. 8, a. 7, ad 1.

Mankind has always given content to its ideas about God on the basis of the circumstances of human history. Life in-and-for-the world feeds our understanding of God, as it were; in essence, Christian religious faith means that our concrete existence is a divine promise of salvation. Only from this life in and for the world does God take on any real content for mankind. If this is overlooked, then one's religious life threatens to turn, not towards the real and living God, but towards a merely notional God; a God, that is, derived from a human experience belonging to the past; in those days the idea had real content, but today, owing to our changed view of man and the world, this content is lost and the notion is just a label which says existentially nothing at all.

Hence it is clearly incorrect to pose the following dilemmas: God or mankind; nature or supernature; human or Christian; flight from the world or concern for the world; direct or mediated relation to God. These things are not opposed to each other in Christianity. So a life presenting itself as directly and exclusively dedicated to God, without human or worldly intermediary, is an unchristian illusion. In spite of good intentions it often leads to a lack of realism in regard to inner structures and human realities, with a certain kind of infantilism as a consequence. Fortunately, concrete experience in the service of mankind— in all kinds of fields—usually turns out in practice to be quite different from its theoretically formulated aims.

The faith-inspired idea that ultimately God is inexpressible therefore seems to me to be of fundamental significance. He becomes nameable by us, takes on real content and comes within the scope of our experience, only on the basis of our life in this world with our fellow men. This means that although we as Christians certainly have a direct and personal relationship with God, we should remember that in its actual concrete content this relationship is *mediated* by the human realities of the world in which we live. Precisely because it is divine, we cannot make a dichotomy between the directness of God's relation to us and the indirect way in which we experience it, through the mediation of secular and human realities in our fellow man (and the church too). Indeed, this is most apparent in the relation between us and Jesus Christ. This relationship is simultaneously inter-human and a *direct* and living relation to God, experienced in faith; for this man *is* God manifest in fully human form, God who desires to be God for us in a human way, God-with-us. Directness and mediation are not mutually exclusive in the relation be-tween God and man; it is in this that God's transcendence is manifest.

Living-for-God thus proceeds indirectly as well as directly, without any need for conflict or tension between these two aspects. Living-for-God also requires a finite, concrete, human objective within this world. For it is only on the basis of our lives in and for the world with our fellow men that we can give any real content to God, without running the danger of coming upon a void. This also means that we could not experience celibacy as mean-ingful in a Christian way if it were not also in some way

a significant human secular possibility for our lives. Otherwise it would indeed be a choice between God and man,
and marriage as a Christian state of life would be, by
definition, only second-rate.

Celibacy, like marriage, is meaningful primarily in human
terms. Both can be lived for the sake of the kingdom of
God. Thus both can be undertaken as states of life that have
Christian significance, too. This means that, in the *first*
instance, Christian celibacy is not the giving up of a natural
value (marriage) for the sake of, and with one's eye on,
a supernatural value. In the first instance celibacy is not a
"supernatural value" but a possible state of life on a human
level, which involves a special dedication to a particular
value. It is not a matter of a choice between God and a
possible marriage partner. God and the marriage partner are
not competitors for our religious love; they do not set up
a choice for our love, as if a true and pure love of God
were possible only if one relinquishes a human partner.
Both Christian marriage and Christian celibacy are values
which, lived with a religious intent, belong to the Christian
supernatural order of salvation. Christian celibacy is the
positive choice of a state of life which is meaningful in itself
in natural and human terms, but is in fact chosen for religious motives and for the sake of religious value because
it possesses an intrinsic suitability. With the phrase "religious motives" I am not reverting to the idea of competition
between God and his creatures; I understand by it the
utmost radical attitude towards God and man and the
world; under "religious value" I do not mean a "worldless

God" (who of course does not exist), but the living God and man in his deepest reality, for this is the kingdom of God.

We have pointed out that the proper suitability of celibacy on a secular level is that it is the expression of a man's desire to concentrate upon a particular value which is worth the dedication of his whole life. Voluntary celibacy implies that a person is so inspired by a particular value that he wants to respond to its call and to put his whole life at its service. This state of life, not necessary but meaningful, evokes in a *special* way a disposition of total availability, in which a person wants to realise a particular human value as a "specialist" wholly devoted to it. Moreover, it is always a value which is fundamental for all mankind. If one puts oneself at the service of this value to such an extent that one wants to remain unmarried, this voluntary celibacy becomes a *sign* expressing a sensitivity to value which exists in all mankind. Such a celibate does not thereby claim a monopoly on this fundamental value, but on the contrary becomes an effective sign and exponent of a quality which ought to flourish in everyone. To the advantage of all, he thus keeps this universal sensitivity-to-value alive and activates it.

Christian celibacy is the same, but the value in question here is religious. Celibacy "for the sake of the kingdom of God" as a Christian state of life guaranteed by the gospel calls attention to the strong drawing-power of religious value. Inspired by its invitation, responding to its appeal, and working under its aegis, a man desires to devote his whole life to it, so much so that he prefers to remain unmarried. He wants to concentrate his efforts in the service of that value, and by this fact alone—for it does not need to be explicitly intended—he becomes a sign in the church and in the world of the sensitivity that men ought to have for religious values. Thus Christian celibacy has an ecclesial as well as a personal significance. Within the church it is a concentrated "sacramentum salutis mundi," an understandable and speaking sign that summons all men to an openness to religious values. In contrast to celibacy—even when experienced in a Christian manner—for the sake of a value which is not directly religious (politics, social work, science, art, etc.), celibacy "for the sake of the kingdom of God" is directly specified by the *religious* value itself.

Therefore we can say that the so-called evangelical guarantee of "Christian celibacy" is nothing other than the fact that Christendom itself, ever since its constitutive phase, has experienced celibacy from the inside out as a state of life that can also be meaningful in a directly *Christian* way. The evangelical guarantee is contained *within* this Christian self-understanding: in the insight of faith that, given the proper nature of celibacy as a humanly significant state of life, Christian life can be lived in a very meaningful way in celibacy; and this can be for the sake of the kingdom of God—i.e., in the religious service of humanity and thus in the service of God, the Founder of the Kingdom.

Religious celibacy clearly has a positive human content, within a manner of living that concentrates as much as possible, in a special way, without undue tension, on the service of the religious value, the most fundamental dimension of life. It is not characterised by a negation, a rejection of human values for the sake of religious or supernatural ones. That would mean a reduction of the religious significance of a Christian life in-and-for the world. Instead, it is a choice between different possibilities for a Christian life. Essentially, it is nevertheless the choice of one meaningful Christian state of life, whereby other meaningful ones are excluded, particularly that which for the majority of Christians is the obvious one, and offers the best opportunities for a Christian life.

The choice itself certainly is a great sacrifice. But what counts is not the sacrifice, or the exclusion of other states of life, but the joyful, positive preference for just this form of Christian existence. Christian celibacy is not the positive choosing of a sacrifice, but the choice of a valuable and fruitful way of Christian living in spite of the realisation that sacrifices are involved in it. Similarly, Christ's *kenôsis*, or self-emptying, was not a by-passing of human values for the sake of supernatural ones, but a choice from among various meaningful messianic possibilities: he chose the way of human helplessness, not that of worldly might and domination. It was the silent way of a fully human manner of life, which he experienced for the sake of his religious mission in the state of celibacy, in order to be completely free for the kingdom of God. Thus Christian celibacy, too, is not a sign of negation, of flight from the world, but of a positive choice: to move towards the future along with the world, that future which is God himself, as the promise of salvation to mankind in history.

Dedication to a value, especially to a religious value,

which transcends our human powers, will certainly imply sufficient sacrifices in and through this faithful service. Besides the choice which involves an exclusion, the sacrifice consequently is the offer of oneself to the value to be served —that is, to God and one's fellow man—for such an unconditional service of love is continually contradicted by human egoism, in ourselves and among others. Self-dispossession is the heart of religious celibacy to the extent that love is—love which does not seek itself but goes outside itself to meet the other. For finite, sinful, and warped human nature, the very essence of love, precisely in its positive value as offering, is not only dedication to God, man, and the world, but at the same time by its very nature a painful self-correction, a sacrifice, a denial of self.

With all this, religious celibacy is on the one hand demythologised—i.e., cut loose from its sacralised wrappings—and on the other hand unfolded in its authentic human and Christian relevance. The human foundation of religious celibacy within the Christian faith thus becomes much clearer. From this basis a renewed appeal can be directed to contemporary man. Nevertheless the fact remains that it is a charisma when someone is so sensitive to religious value and its fundamental importance for all mankind that he wants to place his whole life in its special service in this way. Intrinsically this is a *religious* choice which, in contrast to celibacy for the sake of secular values, is itself directly specified by religious value. In that sense we can say that the *actual* giving up of a human value for the sake of a religious one is implied in this celibacy. (In the same way celibacy for the sake of a suitable activity in the social sphere requires the giving up of a human value.) But this statement is made in a completely different atmosphere from that of the past, and in any case it is still outside the sphere of that distorted dilemma: God or man. This actual giving-up leaves open the possibility of a closer consideration of the sign character of Christian celibacy. In the following pages we will turn our attention to this point. But such an appraisal can add nothing new, and without the foregoing it is even, so it seems to me, irrelevant.

Because people today have discovered more fully than formerly the indirect aspects of the direct experience of God, religious celibacy naturally acquires a new accent. There is a proper stress on the implicitly religious value of the secular life of the faithful, but it brings with it the danger that this secularity will be experienced in a pagan, not in a Christian, light—i.e., without an eschatological perspective. In this context, a life that functions as a relevant sign of the religious dimension of our human existence is more urgent than ever. Christian celibacy can be viewed as a protest against a secularisation that would like to see itself as pagan. The general phenomenology of celibacy (as a special way of giving form to a certain awareness of value, and a vocation enabling one to devote himself entirely and specially to *this* value) becomes focused in Christian celibacy on a Christological, ecclesial, and eschatological significance, the three hallmarks essential to that value for which it was undertaken in the first place: for the sake of the kingdom of God.

DOGMATIC DIMENSIONS OF THIS RELIGIOUS EXPERIENCE

The Christ-Dimension of Religious Celibacy

"For My sake and for the gospel." The man Jesus was un-married, which was not just for no reason, but for the sake of the kingdom of God, which he himself *is* for his fellow men. He enters into a virginal marriage with the church, his bride (Eph 5:32). This is naturally a figure of speech, but it implies that Christ did not come as a social reformer, as someone who devoted himself directly to the secular socio-economic or political order. That was not his "purpose in life." His kingdom is "not of this world": that is the trans-cendent value on which his life was based, and for which he gave up everything else (not his appreciation of these things, but in his *immediate* intent and in the action-radius of his activity, he went beyond them).

We must understand this celibacy from the standpoint of the *man* Jesus, and not—as may easily happen—go back to his divine sonship, and thus see it as a unique occurrence that we cannot base the meaning of *our* celibacy upon. The meaning of the incarnation is precisely—and here lies the short-circuit—that Jesus is the Son of God in humanity. Jesus' being-God becomes evident to us only in his *human* way of reacting to the one whom he called his Father. We should therefore explain his celibacy from the perspective of his humanity, not making a sudden "jump" to his divin-ity. In other words, we ought to refer to his human psy-chology and thus to his value-experience as a man. It is the Man—the Son of God—who is so completely fascinated by the Father and the kingdom of heaven that he voluntarily gives up marriage for it. Jesus' celibacy is not a sort of automatic implication of his being God, but a freely chosen vocation in the service of a realisation of value. Dogmatically—that is, on reflection—we can and must say: in the *man* who is God's Son the absolute value of the divinity incarnates itself in his human will, forming it into a human desire to devote himself entirely and totally to this absolute value; for God has given himself to us as the highest value of human life. Christ does this in a special way, passing up all the other possibilities (those spread before him by Satan in the temptations).

Therefore, in his life Jesus as man has shown us a form of life which can be possible and meaningful for all who feel called to devote themselves entirely and in a special way to this same religious value. The celibacy of Jesus is therefore to be "phenomenologically" understood only on the basis of his *high* valuation of marriage and *even higher* valuation of religious value: the kingdom of God, that which he came to establish. The christological motive, prominent since the fourth century, is a real and meaningful foundation for celibacy that will not let itself be demythologised: by his actual life Jesus as man has shown us a vocational possibility which is meaningful for us.

The Ecclesial Dimension of Christian Celibacy

From this source [Christ] the church, equipped with the gifts of its Founder and faithfully guarding his precepts of charity, humility, and self-sacrifice, receives the mission to proclaim and to spread among all peoples the kingdom of Christ and of God and to be, on earth, the initial budding forth of that kingdom. While it slowly grows, the church strains towards the completed kingdom and, with all its strength, hopes and desires to be united in glory with its King.[11]

With these words the Dogmatic Constitution *Lumen Gentium* recognises the two motives for celibacy in the church: "for my sake and for the gospel," personal adherence to Jesus Christ and apostolic mission based on this foundation. These are the fundamental religious values of the church, as a function of the kingdom of God.

Christian celibacy has an *ecclesial* character. Service to the church can enlist the response of a member to the extent that he gives up everything else for it. His celibacy is a *diakonia* for the church. Likewise, total availability for the service of God and man, a traditional motive for celibacy, takes on its own colour. Church leaders are naturally interested in having some Christians charismatically inspired to remain unmarried in the service of the "double" mission of the church: personal union with Christ and the salvation of mankind. As members of the hierarchy, they can regulate this form of life canonically; and on the other hand, those who want to undertake celibacy for the service of the church can publicly make this known in the presence of the church and have it sanctioned by the church. Related to this ecclesial dimension of Christian celibacy is the question whether the church can promulgate a law of celibacy. It is

[11] Loc. cit., c. 1, n. 5.

clear that the hierarchy cannot oblige anyone to a life that is only understandable as a charisma. Enforced celibacy would be immoral and an encroachment on a man's personal rights. That the church nevertheless reserves her offices for those who feel themselves personally endowed with that charisma is another matter, which will be treated later.

In connection with the ecclesial dimension of celibacy, the Marian aspect also takes a meaningful place in its motivation, having become prominent in the fourth century. But in the spirit of the council it should appear as a truly ecclesial motive.[12] Mary chose the life of a virgin precisely on account of her personal, most intimate union with her Son, Jesus, and his life's work. Thus she is the type of the church and she has truly shown in her actual life the highest possible form of Christian life. Although its explicit justification was perhaps not always accurate, the *practice* of Christian celibacy could be justified in the ancient church on the basis of this intuition of faith into the meaning of the lives of Christ and Mary.

The Eschatological Dimension of Ecclesial Celibacy

Some people think that the eschatological justification of celibacy is outmoded, for they say that we know nothing about the eschaton. The ancient attitude towards the

[12] Loc. cit., c. 8, n. 53 (the blessed virgin and the church), n. 63 (Mary, the type of the church), n. 65 (the church and the emulation of Mary's virtues).

course of the end-fulfilment has been outgrown, and in view of this we will have to describe the eschatological motive more exactly. Compared to the two former motives, this one is not new, but rather an explication of the *inner* tendency towards the future in the mystery of Christ and his church, as that actually exists for us today. So if we knew nothing of the eschata, this would imply, anthropologically, that we also know nothing of the present and our own existence now.

In tradition, this eschatological motive has indeed not always been accurately formulated. Certainly one can hardly consider celibacy in itself as an anticipation of the unmarried condition in the kingdom of heaven (cf. Mt 22: 30). Grace, not celibacy, is an anticipation of life in the kingdom, and married people, too, will share in it. Giving up an actual value (marriage) can hardly be called as such an anticipation of the final *fulfilment* in heaven, where by definition no real giving-up any longer takes place, and certainly not the sacrifice of an undoubted value. Here the Greco-Roman factors have made the true formulation of the eschatological motive more difficult and in fact affected it adversely. Only in so far as celibacy manifests the Christian hope in the coming kingdom of God in a *special* way —even though negatively—is it also in a special way an anticipation of the eschatological kingdom itself, as a particular visible manifestation of the theological (mystic and apostolic) hope; for this hope is a grace-filled grasp of the eschaton ahead of time.

THEOLOGICAL REFLECTION ON THE "EXISTENTIAL INABILITY TO DO OTHERWISE"

Marriage is in the first instance part of man's task of humanising the world and himself together with his fellow men. It is meaningful in terms of this world and considered *in and for itself* it is not a grace-filled, personal union with Christ. Yet it can indeed be a positive expression of this union; faith is not an ideological superstructure built upon worldly realities. But because marriage *per se* has a secular significance, the grace of God can be visible in it only in a veiled manner; the marriage of unbelievers can therefore *look* the same as that of Christians. Yet the kingdom of God transcends this world, although it needs to incarnate itself in all dimensions of the secular. Man's acceptance of God's redeeming grace, as it takes place in the process of justification, is itself a pure grace of God. This divine act of justification is an *eschatological* reality: the living God himself *for us*. The secular is by definition not the reality *out of which* salvation can arise. Salvation lies in God, the transcendent reality. Thus God's redeeming grace is an eschatological event, which becomes a visible *reality within* this world in and through our free, graced response.

Justification is accomplished in a human act but not by human power, nor is it an element in the process of cultural humanisation. The kingdom of God, the dominion of God become visible in our human world, does not arise from this world, though it is within it. It comes about by an ecstatic gesture, in which a man rises beyond himself, beyond the limits of his worldly human existence seen as meaningful in secular terms, in order to be able to accept grace *as the grace of God*. This acceptance of grace is at the same time a supreme act of self-emptying in which, by virtue of grace, grace is accepted precisely as being "not of or from this world," as not springing from any worldly value whatsoever. Only in this acceptance is grace manifest as a grace that has come into history.

Especially since Karl Rahner's consideration of this point,[13] it is often said that celibacy "for the sake of the kingdom of God" brings this world-transcending character of grace to us in a relevant *sign*. I think that this is correct, if at least it is considered as an aspect of the phenomenological structure of celibacy for the sake of the realisation of a value, as described earlier. Celibacy as such is not a supernatural value but a state of life that is meaningful in human terms. Without this perspective, Rahner's explanation seems to be too much of a verbal construction, purely theoretical, which nevertheless runs the risk of posing a false dilemma in the married person's relation with God. Celibacy is a choice, but it is a choice between two possible states of Christian life, not *formally* between a natural and a supernatural value. Because the value in question is as such a religious one, the choice of this kind of celibacy actually implies that one gives up a human value because one wants to realise another value. Any voluntary celibacy implies a

[13] In particular in "Über die evangelische Räte," in *Geist und Leben* 17 (1964), 17–37, and to a lesser extent in "Zur Theologie der Entsagung," in *Schriften zur Theologie*, v. 3, Einsiedeln 1959–   , 61–72.

giving-up, but celibacy "for the sake of the kingdom of God" concerns religious value in itself: that is its specifying characteristic. Directly religious celibacy thereby acquires a transcendent quality, incomprehensible from a purely secular point of view: the transcendence of the religious dimension itself. *Religious* celibacy is for this world an insoluble question mark; that is why it brings (negatively, in and through that actual giving-up) the eschatological world-transcendence or gratuity of grace into visible expression. This can be called a necessary accompaniment of Christian celibacy: negatively (that is, by not marrying in order to be in a position to undertake a special task) it serves to emphasise the special, concentrated application to the religious dimension of our lives. This celibacy *is* the special application to this sphere, and therefore a sign and exponent of this religious dimension as an appeal directed to all men.

But we cannot say that this celibacy is an unambiguous expression of it and that Christian married life is always an ambiguous expression because marriage in itself, viewed in terms of this world, already has meaning on the human level and therefore cannot have this reference to the kingdom of God as its specifying characteristic. For not only does grace reach objective expression equally well in married life, but on the other hand psychoanalysis has taught us that so-called "religious celibacy" can also be ambiguous. But this does not do away with the fact that in authentic religious celibacy a human life is placed in a special way in the service of religious value, and thus becomes a sign and expression of the religious dimension of life, precisely as the gratuitous gift of God, which cannot be the result of human endeavour. Thus celibacy, also as sign, is a special charisma.

One may perhaps ask oneself why there should be any need for such a speaking sign of transcendent grace within our world and the church. Moreover, why should it be *better* to give form to the transcendence of grace, rather than to its redemptive leavening of the great secular values? Should we not rather dedicate ourselves wholeheartedly in faith and hope to the Christian promotion of the great secular values? In any case, this thought protects those who are single "for the sake of the kingdom of God" from disdain and leads them to a positive recognition of the other authentic Christian way of life: Christian living in and for the world. The two forms of Christian life are complementary and essentially imply the positive recognition on the part of each that the other form is necessary for the church too. Both forms ought to be *mutually present* to each other, for otherwise the single life is a sign seen by no one, a silent *hortus conclusus*, not a sign in the world.

But the fact that church and world really need such a sign becomes clear to anyone who recalls that celibacy reveals the heart of religious life-values—namely, that only in self-transcendence does the grace of the kingdom of God come to us, and not through our own achievement or through our human dedication to secular goals. The religious celibate reserves his vital attention for the very heart of the kingdom of God, without whose living presence in this world *Christian* promotion of worldly values threatens indeed to become an empty slogan. Celibacy *purely for religious* reasons cannot be placed within the framework of human endeavour to realise secular values, nor is it understandable in these terms (although afterwards its fruitful resonance in the realisation of such values becomes apparent). Celibacy directly for the realisation of *secular* values is understandable in human terms. But celibacy "for the sake of the kingdom of God" is incomprehensible in these terms; it is a living appeal that sows unrest and draws attention to the fact that the deepest fulfilment of human life does not lie in the things of this world. Thus for the secular world and for other Christians, Christian celibacy is a continuous summons which makes the heart of the kingdom of God and of the church visible in human history and places it in the midst of the world.

But this celibacy only has meaning for the person himself, and therefore for the world and the church, to the extent that the sign is inwardly charged with the reality that it signifies; in other words, that the unmarried person is caught up into the spell of the kingdom of God. Then one can say—according to the dialectic of human "sign activity" —that the very nature of (Christian) celibacy is in a special way inwardly *suited* to the broadening and deepening in a special way of personal union with Christ and the apostolate. Through this round-about means we come to a re-evaluation of a traditional motive which has not always been properly justified, namely, that celibacy removes the impediments to an intensive love of God and man, and is therefore a freeing of love. In this perspective, this motivation loses the taint of Hellenistic dualism and an outmoded view of man and the world. It also suggests how careful we should be with all-too-facile conclusions based on our altered view of man and our deeper appreciation of secular values.

4

CELIBACY AND THE MINISTRY

THE FUNDAMENTAL INSPIRATION
COMMON TO PRIESTHOOD AND CELIBACY

When priesthood and celibacy confront each other against the background of the gospel, the Christian possibility of celibacy in its positive significance will clearly present itself as a real divine *invitation* for anyone who accepts evangelical office in the church. The affinity between the charisma of celibacy and the priestly ministry is in itself phenomenologically suggestive. For the pattern fundamental to them both is a total and special availability for the service of God and men. The official "setting apart for the gospel of God" (Rom 1:1) easily allows itself, phenomenologically speaking, to be translated in terms of religious celibacy.

Clerical Celibacy According to Vatican II

On December 7, 1965, the Decree on the Ministry and Life of Priests was solemnly approved. This decree sees clerical celibacy in the light of "perfect and perpetual continence for the sake of the kingdom of heaven."[1] It is explicitly stated that celibacy is *not essentially* bound up with priest-

[1] C. 3, n. 16.

hood.[2] Therefore the council evidently does not consider the eastern practice of having married priests as second-rank. Nevertheless the emphasis is placed on the "many-faceted suitability" of celibacy and priesthood. This religious celibacy is at the same time a sign and a stimulus for pastoral charity, and a special source of spiritual fecundity in the world.[3] The great desirability of clerical celibacy is evident from the official mission of the priest, who devotes himself entirely and completely "to the service of a new humanity which Christ, the victor over death, has raised up through his spirit in the world and which has its origin 'not of blood, nor of the will of the flesh, nor of the will of man, but of God' (Jn 1:13)."[4] To be a sign of the transcendence of grace is therefore explicitly affirmed in this decree; also one finds confirmed here the already analysed motive of giving oneself to God *"more easily* with an undivided heart" and likewise devoting oneself "more freely in him and through him to the service of God and men."[5] The decree is careful not to speak of a monopoly of service to the kingdom of God and of sonship to God experienced by the celibate: repeatedly it says "more easily," "more freely," "more expeditiously." Thus priests witness to the bridal relationship between Christ and his church. They are "a living sign of the world to come, by a faith and charity already made present, in which the children of the resurrection neither marry nor take wives."[6]

[2] Loc. cit.   [3] Loc. cit.
[4] Loc. cit.   [5] Loc. cit.
[6] Loc. cit.

From these quotations it is evident that the anti-sexual sentiment which clearly played a part in the patristic period is completely absent in this decree: it concerns the purely biblical celibacy "for the sake of the kingdom of God," brought into relation with the proper nature of ecclesiastical office. It is on account of this close connection with priesthood, at one time only advisory, that it was later made into a law by the Latin church for all who receive sacred orders.[7] For priests at least (no longer for deacons) the council confirms this law anew:

This legislation, pertaining to those who are destined for the priesthood, this holy synod again approves and confirms, fully trusting this gift of the Spirit so fitting for the priesthood of the New Testament, freely given by the Father, provided that those who participate in the priesthood of Christ through the sacrament of Orders—and also the whole Church—humbly and fervently pray for it.[8]

The decree acknowledges that religious celibacy is difficult for human nature, but that "this outstanding gift of the Father" is too important for the church to have the traditional legislation changed because of these difficulties. All kinds of proposals and amendments to weaken the new confirmation of the law of celibacy were rejected. Indeed, because of orders from a higher authority the council fathers could not discuss the celibacy law in public, but

[7] Loc. cit.
[8] Loc. cit.

written interventions were allowed and were studied by the commission concerned. Finally the council all but unanimously agreed with the approval or rejection by the commission of the amendments that had been considered.

It is clear that this conciliar decree does not wish to make any distinction between the celibacy of religious orders and that of priests, at least not insofar as its content is concerned. Although the decree breaks through the traditional, purely "cultic" image of the priest and separates priestly holiness from the traditional monastic ideal, the celibacy of priests is formulated in the same words as that of religious in the decree on the renewal of religious life: on both sides, biblical celibacy "for the sake of the kingdom of God" is spoken of, without recourse to the (pagan) motive of cultic purity.

Reflection and Problems

The priesthood is an *official* vocation in the church: "As the Father has sent me, even so I send you" (Jn 20:21; 17:18). But the direct parallel of this is "As the Father has loved me, so have I loved you" (Jn 15:9). The *Agapè*, God's disinterested sacrificing love, appearing to us in human form in Jesus, is the horizon of priestly life. This love binds the man, the priest, in Christ to God in such a way that in the same movement it likewise directs him towards his fellow man. In this connection it seems to me that the definition given in scripture of Jesus, the high priest, is most significant: "anthroopos Jèsous Christous, ho dous heauton" (1 Tim 2:6): "The man Christ Jesus, the self-giving one." It does not say, "who gives or has given himself," but "ho dous," used substantively: the giving one. Christ *is* self-gift, to the Father and to mankind; out of this love he also sends the priest to men, and for those two well-known motives: "for my sake," and "for the gospel," to bind them personally to Christ and to bring them the good news. Thus it is a mission to mankind, a being together with men, but in order to turn their attention towards that Other, "on behalf of men in relation to God" (Heb 5:1). By his vocation the priest is focused on the essence of the church, which is the beginning of the kingdom of God, which is not of this world and yet has consequences for the *Christian* promotion of secular values. As pastor of souls the priest therefore assists the faithful both in their transcendence of self towards God, and in their efforts to order their lives in this world in a Christian manner.

In this light the official ministry has of its nature a special affinity with the evangelical content of celibacy. The priest's duty concerns the *religious values* in human life, to which he does not devote himself as a neutral functionary, but which he personally supports as prophet too. The priest (the bishop with his college of presbyters and deacons who shared his ministry) was viewed in the ancient church as the "image"—i.e., the manifestation in mystery of Christ the high priest on one hand, and on the other hand of the local community of the faithful, whose pastor he was. Patterning himself after Christ, the priest had to show in his actual life what ought to take form in the congregation.

Thus official ministry and private life were attuned to each other in him. The personal adherence of the priest to Christ (in collegial union with the bishop and fellow priests) is concretely the *sacramentum* of the bond between the local congregation and God, and of the community-building love of this group in the church and the world. Of this basic reality his strictly official services are only the concrete manifestation on the formally official level (service of the word, administration of the sacraments, and leadership of the brotherhood).

If this priestly service becomes a life project—that is, a full-time function as is the case in the western church—it intrinsically includes an invitation to religious celibacy, as a special way of being available for the service of God and mankind: a positive possibility of the highest significance, a real divine call, and not a strict demand. In itself, the vocation to the priesthood is another thing than that to celibacy. Nevertheless in both the eastern and western church that inward invitation has been understood, and from the beginning many ministers have spontaneously answered it.

Yet certainly the western church has gone further than this and made celibacy obligatory. Does it have the competence and jurisdiction to do this?

As a charisma, celibacy can only be accepted in freedom, never directly or indirectly imposed, not even by the ecclesiastical hierarchy. The priestly office itself could certainly be imposed upon the faithful by church authority on the basis of Christian obedience. But in such a case, church authority could never impose celibacy as the condition for the reception of orders, for that would be an indirect way of making a charisma obligatory. In actuality, the church leaves her members free in their choice of the ministry. Can the church in this case then decree that it will ordain only those who feel themselves personally called to religious celibacy, and in that sense establish a *law* of celibacy?

We have seen that Christian celibacy is an ecclesial reality, controlled by church leaders and regulated by them in its concrete form. Moreover, the highest authority in the church can indeed put every stress on the inner affinity between Christian celibacy and ministry, and thus make the inward, though not necessary, but still most meaningful connection between them as a matter of obligation. The highest church authority has the right to confer the ministry (which the *hierarchy* ultimately entrusts to some of the faithful) only on those who freely accept or have accepted religious celibacy. So the eastern church chooses its bishops almost entirely from monks; moreover, the eastern as well as the western church denies marriage to those already ordained who continue to exercise their ministry. Although in practice this may be tolerated in a few of the smaller eastern churches, at least for deacons and priests, nevertheless the principle itself is unanimously accepted. *In this respect* the attitude of the universal church is uniform. The Christian intuition underlying it can be elaborated as follows: the episcopacy is the fullness of priesthood and hence carries with it in optimal form the inner invitation to religious celibacy. This invitation remains in diminished yet real form in the presbyterate and the diaconate. The fact that at this point the eastern and

western churches separate to some extent can partly be
accounted for because the presbyterate and the diaconate
in the east are not always full-time functions. This all but
removes from the ministry its inner invitation to religious
celibacy, because this is precisely a life commitment
whereby one devotes himself entirely and completely to
the realisation of religious values.

In any case there is this difference between the east and
the west: in the east it is *normal* that men who have *already*
been married are ordained deacon or priest while retaining
a full married life. In the Latin church this is still an exception for priests. For deacons, it has become possible since
the Constitution on the Church. The intrinsic appeal of the
"apostolic ministry" to religious celibacy is less strong in
this diminished form of ecclesiastical office. On the other
hand, it makes sense that married life, too, should be open
to the church's minister, who has to show in his actual life
what the community of the faithful ought to be. This
exemplification of Christian life in one's own family is
explicitly recorded in the Pastoral Epistles describing married ministers (1 Tim 3:1–5). In the east today, the fact
that there are married and unmarried ministers as a group
can exemplify more completely the Christian life in its two
fundamental aspects, eschatological holiness and Christian
living in-and-for the world—a possibility which the western church still lacks. Yet in its totality western Christendom is more "worldly minded" and more engaged in
material things, in spite of the abundance of *signa* of religious celibacy, than eastern Christendom is. From this it is
evident that the mere *number* of "signs" of world-tran-

scendence does not automatically give to Christianity an authentic eschatological character.

One can also consider the problem from the ministers' own point of view, and say that for some of them to be able to fall back again and again into the safety of home and family is a necessary condition of their devoting themselves heart and soul to a value, including a religious one. It should be remembered that this situation also requires of the marriage partner a special openness to the vocation of the other. *This* aspect is too often forgotten in the appeal for "married priests." The case is considered only from the point of view of the man, the priest. Moreover, people often look only at the difficulties in the celibate life of the priest, and then confront this with an ideal (sometimes even purely idyllic) concept of marriage. The difficult task which inevitably falls to the lot of the priest's wife seems to me an essential aspect of the problem. The difficulties and suspicions that can arise in the married life of a doctor, for example, can serve as a parallel.

That the church in the west applies the eastern legislation for bishops likewise to the "priesthood of the second rank" (the presbyterate, according to the words of the ordination ceremonial), shows that it sees the presbyterate principally as a full-time function which takes up the whole of a person's life, and that it chooses as priests only those who model their priestly life after that of the episcopate.

Nevertheless there are problems here. Some people think that the *law* of celibacy is strictly an *obligation* to celibacy. From the foregoing, it appears that on close inspection this is an unfortunate, formally inaccurate expression, strictly speaking. The church obliges no one to celibacy. It simply cannot do so; or if it tried, it would be overstepping its authority. This is evident in the canon providing that no one may receive higher orders unless he has previously stated (since 1931, in writing) that he *freely* embraces religious celibacy. And on the other hand, no individual member of the church has the *right* to an ecclesiastical office. Admission to the ministry is concretely, at least in the final instance, a matter for the church's hierarchy to decide (cf. Acts 1:24), guided by the Spirit (Acts 20:28). If a member were able to claim the *right* to office in the church, the church could not attach the requirement of celibacy to it, for that would be an immoral compulsion and indirectly an actual obligation of celibacy. But the Latin church desires that even the ordinary priesthood (in principle) be exercised in the form of religious celibacy, which is inwardly inspired by the nature of the priesthood, as a life commitment which, though not necessary to it, can be highly meaningful for it. Yet this regulation—the law of celibacy—requires a still closer examination that goes deeper than the question of church authority.

DIALECTICAL TENSION BETWEEN THE DATUM OF "EXISTENTIAL INABILITY TO DO OTHERWISE" AND THE JURIDICAL LAW OF CELIBACY

The idea that freely willed celibacy for the more intense realisation of an important human value is phenomenologically highly meaningful, though not necessary, is a conceptual schematising, which impoverishes to some extent the proper content of the actual experience itself. To one who, caught up in the spell of the kingdom of God, spontaneously and without counting the cost gives up everything, the expression "highly meaningful, though not necessary" seems psychologically like only a pale reflection of his personal experience. For him it certainly is a question of "existential inability to do otherwise," as expressed in the *eunouchia* passage in Matthew. Such an experience of reality does not lend itself to a precise formulation in juridical terms of "obligation," "no obligation," or "highly desirable." The statements of scripture concern precisely this area of vital experience that transcends questions of must and must not. The ministry belongs in a sphere of charismatic enthusiasm, and is in fact one of the many different manifestations of it. In scripture, too, it is not the giving up and the sacrifice which are stressed, but the overwhelming joy of finding the great treasure; all the rest, however valuable it may be, is simply forgotten beside that. In such a situation, when someone is swept off his feet by the new experience, is there any sense in asking, "Does it have to be this way?" Similarly, we don't ask a girl who has just been married and embraces her bridegroom, then bursts into tears of joy or does other silly things, whether these are now necessary or useful. Whoever has gone through the experience himself knows that for him this "necessity" is more compelling than any command or law whatsoever. Such an experience of the kingdom of God intrinsically demands that reaction and no other, although we know that there are also other kinds of rich experiences of the kingdom of God. If we now start to *analyse* this enthusiasm and ask the sober question, "Does one *have to* give up everything for it?" we already put ourselves *outside* the original experience. Then the analysing, reflective intellect can only say: no, *per se* it is not necessary, but it is a possibility with great depth of meaning. Thus the reflection can never come up to the experience. Faced with the evidence of the experience itself, the formulation is but a feeble stammer.

For the same reason, the law of celibacy (which as law is by its very nature formulated) also stands in dialectical tension with the experience: in this law something which is an inner logic spontaneously assented to by a man who as minister lives under the spell of God's kingdom in a special way is strictly imposed as an obligation for all ministers.

A Common Psychological Pattern

First of all, it is evident that the fundamental archetype of this phenomenon appears rather frequently in religious life. Psychologists of religion have analysed the anthropological structures of related phenomena, for example, fasting. Lack of appetite is something that can *happen to* a person because of certain experiences: for example, a death, a fearful expectation, great tension—all these are experiences that take our appetite away. Now, it is noteworthy that many religions prescribe a ritual of fasting when a death occurs. The Christian religion, too, prescribes fasting for times of great religious expectation (Advent; preparation for Easter). The psychological pattern that functions here seems clear. On the basis of the psychic experience that one undergoes at bereavement, or in tension because of a coming event, an experience so intense that appetite disappears, one tries to evoke a similar experience—even if the appetite is not diminished by *voluntarily* bringing about the otherwise spontaneous effect of such an experience: voluntarily one does not eat, one fasts. By this symbolic activity—voluntary fasting—people try as it were by means of the "consequence" to induce in themselves *the original experience.* Psychologically, the various kinds of fasting in Israel are understandable in these terms. Sometimes people are so upset over their misdeeds that they lose their appetite. The fact that David fasted so intensely after his sin with Bathsheba was such an *original* experience (2 Sam 12:16), not the observance of a previous law. He was greatly disturbed and could not eat; his fasting itself was his deeply experienced sorrow. Out of such basic experiences, the later Jewish laws developed—for example, the great fast upon the Day of Atonement (Num 29:7). By taking upon oneself voluntarily the "spontaneous effect" of sorrow and a deep need of conscience, one tries to evoke the personal awareness of sin (which is not yet so intense that it takes away the appetite); in human weakness, but with confidence in God, one strives for the original authentic experience, one carves out an area in which this can develop psychologically, and as it were makes itself possible. That which in the original experience is a "spontaneous effect" and "inner logic" (not eating) thus becomes transposed into an inwardly appropriate means of recalling or intensifying the authentic experience. Also the eucharistic fast before Communion did not, historically, develop out of respect for the sacrament or asceticism. It is rooted in the same anthropological pattern: it expresses expectation and is a way of preparation. The original experience of being so intent upon a coming event that one forgets to eat is imitated in symbolical religious activity, so that by voluntarily fasting, we might really come to live in expectation of the eucharistic event. The experience becomes *realisable* in the sign, so that we focus ourselves upon the authentic experience: the spontaneous human way of expressing an authentic longing for a true actual experience.

The same basic anthropological pattern operates in the law of celibacy. The "existential inability to do otherwise" —on the level of moral obligation weakened to "not necessary but most meaningful"—is set down as a law of celibacy. Because the ministry inwardly calls one to celibacy —which only forces itself upon those who experience the overwhelming discovery of the kingdom of God, for example, the apostles—the church imposes the "spontaneous effect" of that experience on anyone who wants to become a priest, but perhaps possesses this experience only in germ as yet, in order that *within it* and *by means of it* he will come indeed to a true religious experience in which alone the practice of the ministry finds its deepest meaning. This imposed celibacy must make it *actually* possible to realise that authentic religious value-experience of the kingdom of God, in the service of which the priest stands. Thus the law and the focus-on-the-experience stand in a dialectical tension. Only by looking from one angle can we speak meaningfully of an "obligation," because for a person who has gone through this original experience of grace in his own life, the concept of "obligation" is meaningless: existentially he cannot do otherwise. He who does not have this spontaneous experience, but voluntarily accepts the ministry and therefore clerical celibacy, devotes himself, in full confidence in God's grace, through the acceptance of the celibacy law with special intensity to the kingdom of God. Thereby he at least gives evidence of his desire to enter in a special way into the realm of grace from which that celibacy intrinsically arises. This attitude is a call to God out of human weakness, to come under his spell in such a way that existentially celibacy becomes the only possible vocation. Personally I can experience my own priestly and monastic celibacy in no other way than in the form of *continual beseeching*, that *existentially* I may not be able to do otherwise.

Thus if the church recognises a law of celibacy for priests, this law is only the juridical translation of an anthropological pattern, functioning on the basis of the original experience of an apostle of Christ who, overwhelmed by finding the "hidden treasure," has become blind to the objectively still open possibility of married life. The law of celibacy is the juridical exponent of the inner logic of a deep religious experience which the church's ministers above all should show in their actual life. The law of celibacy is the church's attempt to *reactivate* the reception of holy orders into that original experience which intrinsically calls forth the spontaneous practice of celibacy.

Ambivalence in This Basic Psychological Pattern

Dogmatically and anthropologically, the relationships between charisma and law are plain in the western church too. But every human symbolic activity is ambivalent and can lead to formalism. Given the law of celibacy, it is possible that candidates for the priesthood, who really desire the ministry, accept the celibacy connected with it only because they have to. Of course this is not the purpose of the law, but it forms a drawback to it that is not to be underestimated, especially in times and places where the priesthood is also a socially desirable position. Anyone who does not *primarily* and explicitly want to give himself to religious celibacy at his ordination inevitably sows the seed of later misfortune. Celibacy is not the sort of thing that one can take on because one has to along with something else. In spite of all the care that can be taken in the education and training for the priesthood, the law of celibacy in the concrete still produces problems.[9] On the other hand,

---

[9] Even aside from the hard treatment of priests who have been stranded for years, and cannot live a good Christian life because ordination is juridically an impediment to a valid marriage. This is also apart from concordats (in Italy, even a part of the civil law) which deny the most minimal civil government employment (even that of porter) to priests who are canonically irregular, so that they are often found trapped in grievous need. Then too, not a few of these "fallen priests" should not be considered ethically at fault, but rather they are the

the number of failures, however many there may be, are
not *by themselves* the norm of clerical celibacy, any more
than marriage is considered meaningless because it provides
the opportunity for adultery. Moreover, such failures are
often to be ascribed to inadequate sexual and emotional formation.[10] Celibacy not only requires a deep religious moti-

---

eventual result of psychological inhibitions or social maladjustment; or,
if there is no neurotic or pathological background, their condition is
the consequence of a radically mistaken choice of vocation. But all these
canonical regulations stem from a previous era, when in all areas of life
people had more confidence in disciplinary regulations than in risk-
taking love. Pope Paul VI is effecting fundamental changes in these
matters.

[10] Fidelity to one's pledged word, especially in religious matters, is, it
seems to me, something sacred in which relationships of justice weigh
very heavily. By this I don't mean to deny that the pledged word also
carries with it a whole casuistry (for example, the real possibility of a
fundamentally mistaken vocational choice; neurotic, pathological, or all
sorts of other factors can later on create an impossible situation, humanly
speaking, and from a Christian point of view, even though the pledged
word was freely given). Moreover, let us not forget that the present
celibacy crisis, insofar as it is connected with the withdrawal from
priestly ministry, also has many non-theological aspects. Priests' abandon-
ment of their ministry and the return of religious to lay life is not a
socially senseless adventure in our times, which in the church and
society of former times it certainly was. In this sense, the "social barrier"
has been broken, whereas formerly the "misfit priests" hardly ever made
the break to the outside world because they would not be accepted
there. This seems to be only an extrinsic, unqualified difference between
then and now. Still, the possibility of being socially accepted is for some
a *new temptation*, peculiar to our times, in which the example of others
plays a part. From the outside, one cannot make any general judgement
about individual cases. An important factor is certainly the inability to
come to terms with the relation between world and church, or between

vation, which must not be too rashly presupposed, but also presumes a normal biological and psychological substratum, so that the psychic integration of the unmarried person and his normal emotional development are not hindered. Religious celibacy requires a characteristic emotional and social "Christian culture."

We have seen too that throughout church history there has been opposition to a law of celibacy for the ministry. Each age brings forth its own point of view on this question. In the past, on account of the now outdated ideas about marriage and sexuality, today's objections were unknown. Then the justification for celibacy was positively based on incorrect motives which we now experience as insufficient. So today, through what we can call "loss of function" of the motivation, the justification of religious celibacy has become psychologically more tenuous for many people: they miss the former handy (pseudo) supports. Moreover, strong Christian enthusiasm which formerly found an outlet only in religious celibacy now finds a field of action in marriage as well, re-evaluated in Christian thought. The quantitative decrease of those who are single "for the sake of the kingdom of God" therefore seems normal to me, and is in itself not at all a symptom of religious laxity. Indeed, to the extent that the whole people of God are becoming more actively aware of their Christian duties, the need for priests also decreases. If one thinks of

---

the secular and the religious, because it is just here that *religious* celibacy, as a specific affirmation of the world-transcending character of grace, becomes problematic first of all.

how many priests (especially in the past) devoted three-quarters of their day to layman's work—which could often have been technically better done by laymen—then it seems to me that in our part of the world the suggestion of removing celibacy so as to increase the recruitment of priests is hardly reasonable. Not only unchristian, but even more, touching the very heart of Christendom, as I see it, is the tendency to dismiss celibacy as meaningless in any real human and Christian way, seeing it only as a consequence of a superseded dualistic and unreal idea of God and mankind. This point of view has never been significantly established to any extent, but now more than ever the complementary character of religious celibacy as a human reality is apparent, just when we are emphasising a *rightly ordered* Christian enthusiasm for the world (which yet must never lose sight of the real sin and ambiguity that can exist within the secular). It is not for nothing that religious celibacy has been rediscovered in Protestantism in the Reformation of the present day.

In a concluding chapter, then, we must consider the question of whether the desire for a change in western canonical law is justified from a pastoral and theological point of view.

5

PASTORAL AND THEOLOGICAL CONSEQUENCES FOR THE FUTURE

Our hermeneutic appraisal of clerical celibacy and its motivation has led to some suggestive dogmatic and historical conclusions. It is apparent that in fact the explicit Christian justification for celibacy sprang from the human self-understanding that had already been developed before the coming of Jesus (the "heathen" Greco-Roman motives for chastity). Only gradually did these become purified—down to the present day—through an interpretation of self inspired by Jesus' earthly life. The present changes in our view of mankind, the world, and God, far from showing that religious celibacy is meaningless, have on the contrary clarified exceedingly its deeper meaning for the sake of the kingdom of God. Specifically, the possibility of celibacy for the more intense realisation of important human values provided a fruitful starting-point.

The theology on Christ, the church, and the ministry shows that even at the phenomenological level there is a meaningful *inner* relationship between evangelical office in the church and evangelical celibacy. The ministry, itself a charisma, contains within itself a positive call to the voluntary acceptance of religious celibacy. On the level of conceptual schematising, we can say that although this relationship is intrinsic and invites one towards its realisation, nevertheless it does not necessarily *demand* this realisation in each individual case. In itself, marriage is thus not an obstacle to ordination, an insight that is shared by both the eastern and the western church.

The inner relationship between ministry and celibacy is on the other hand such a sovereign invitation that the church, in the east as well as in the west, admits to the fullness of the ministry, the episcopate, only those who personally accept the charisma of celibacy and, with the help of grace, a *special*, lifelong and total consecration to the religious values of the kingdom of God and of the church. The difference between the eastern and the Latin canonical regulations for the state of life of the lesser forms of ministry (diaconate and presbyterate) indicates that for them the positive invitation to religious celibacy, while real and meaningful, is to some extent less urgent. Reflecting upon these facts, we have reached the following conclusions.

(1) Western theology is still discussing whether or not there is a promise of celibacy (possibly implicit) connected with the reception of holy orders, even the subdiaconate, which does not strictly belong to office in the church, but in the west is considered as the actual entrance to the diaconate and the priesthood. Thus there is a certain ambiguity in the actual situation. The structure of this church regulation (the law of celibacy) should not in any case give rise to one's acceptance of celibacy as something that

merely "goes along with" ordination. As long as this regulation exists, a complete restructuring of the formation of
seminarians ought to express in a better way the charismatic significance of celibacy—and the psycho-social and
emotional integration connected with it; indeed, it ought
to make it psychologically possible.

(2) The historical situation of world and church suggests that it would make sense from a Christian point of
view to admit married persons not only to the diaconate
(the Constitution *Lumen Gentium* already allows this), but
also to the priesthood, in addition to having unmarried
priests. For *individual* cases this has been allowed repeatedly, thus recognising the need to a certain extent. Also for
ecumenical reasons we can certainly expect that this form
of priesthood in the western church will become more
frequent in the near future, whether in conjunction with
the present law of celibacy, from which dispensations may
frequently be given for those already married, or whether
by taking over the Trullan law of the eastern church which
is still in force—i.e., that those who are already married can
become deacons or priests. This last alternative would leave
untouched the western legislation that a deacon or priest
ordained when still unmarried may not marry later.

(3) On the other hand, for pastoral and theological
reasons, I would plead that the doors of mercy be opened
wide for priests who, for whatever reason, find that they
have made a mistake in their vocational choice of clerical
celibacy, so that (without further exercise of office) they
could build up once more a truly human and Christian life

in marriage. That such a charitable attitude might, as people say, open the floodgates, seems to me to be an unchristian fear which has little confidence in the charismatic attraction of religious celibacy.

(4) Some people would evidently like to go a step further: they strive for the removal of celibacy for candidates for the "secular" priesthood. What shall we think of this?

Pastoral theology is more than dogmatic theology. Rooted in the past, standing in the present, dogmatic theology can sketch the *possibilities* for the future: the church may take this or that direction. On the contrary, pastoral theology says: in view of the present situation in the world and the church, we must go in this direction and not that one; it must have the "spirit of discernment" in order to make a concrete decision and to formulate an *ethical imperative* from the signs of the times, in the service of the church and its hierarchical leadership. Our dogmatic analysis, too, therefore needs to be supplemented with pastoral-theological judgements.

Since the connection between celibacy and ministry is not in itself *compulsory*, to speak in abstract formal terms, we cannot foresee whether, for priests and deacons, the church will ever insist only upon the positive invitation or inner appeal to conscience when candidates for ordination decide whether or not to accept religious celibacy. Dogmatic theology cannot at least exclude this possibility *a priori*. Moreover, in the east it is a reality, though only to a slight extent. Close questioning of eastern bishops, Uniate and Orthodox (during the council), about the life of seminarians made me see that in the east, the possibility of married or single life is open to seminarians before their ordination to the diaconate. There are at least a few seminaries in which students who still want to marry, or who are actually engaged, are accepted.

The Second Vatican Council has officially affirmed the relationship of affinity—that is, the suitability of celibacy for the priesthood; on *this point* there was full unanimity among the bishops of the east and west. The sharpest episcopal intervention concerning celibacy did not attack this idea of affinity, nor even the *law;* it was only a fervent plea that those *already married* should be ordained in much larger numbers, considering the present pastoral needs. When the council reaffirmed the *law* of celibacy, an estimated 400 of the 2,200 bishops who voted for it expressed their desire for some adjustment of it in such a way that the church would be less tied down to it in the future. This is suggested in one of the amendments (*modus*) which was turned in:

In spite of the great difficulties in which the law of celibacy places many priests, the council sees no pressing reasons to make any changes in it now.

The conciliar statement of the *theological* affinity idea cannot be ignored; on the other hand, a certain doubt is growing among the bishops about the pastoral appropriateness of the *law* of celibacy.

Moreover, the council wanted clearly to dissociate or distinguish the priestly state of life from monastic spirituality, yet it continued to connect clerical celibacy with the "existential inability to do otherwise" that lies hidden in being "incapable of marriage for the sake of the kingdom of God." The latter is a biblical affirmation; the inner affinity between this fact and the acceptance of a church office is, however, not biblical, except in a certain restricted sense: the bible nowhere states this connection *explicitly*. Or perhaps it does, for according to many exegetes, when Jesus stated the fact of "those who are unmarriageable for the sake of the kingdom of God" he was thinking first of all of the apostles and his closest disciples. If this is so, the relation of affinity would be explicitly set forth. And even if Jesus was not thinking specifically of the apostles, we have still not exhausted the biblical resources on this point. Other Catholic beliefs which are not explicitly stated in the bible can still be "biblical" (see the Dogmatic Constitution on Divine Revelation).

I am not maintaining that the council has explicitly stated this idea of affinity to be an element of faith; but its affirmation of this relationship is the main point of the conciliar statements on clerical celibacy. Moreover, it is not just a matter of a purely psychological or anthropological affinity (from that angle one could just as well affirm a connection between office in the church and being married), but rather it is a theological affinity, apparent from the *essence* of the ministry compared with the *essence* of "being unmarried for the sake of the kingdom of God."

That is the fundamental tenor of the conciliar statement; and the *essence* of these two is biblical. Consequently the idea of their affinity is itself a biblical datum, even though it cannot be so maintained by exegetics alone.

It is striking that the affinity which the conciliar decree on the ministry and life of priests sees between religious celibacy and priesthood is declared only after the three essential functions of the priesthood have been explained: the service of the world, the administration of the sacraments, and the leadership of the community of the faithful (chap. II, n. 4–6). In these three functions lies the essence of the priestly service of the kingdom of God, even though this threefold service can take on all kinds of concrete forms according to pastoral needs. The essence of the church's ministry is not identical with its historically developed manifestations. Therefore one should not connect the theological idea of affinity with an outdated formulation of priestly function; according to the conciliar decree, it is essential to the priestly function itself. The experience of value which leads one to choose the ministry, and the experience of value which is fundamental to religious celibacy, touch each other very closely. The conciliar decree did well not to separate the *ministry* and the *life* of the priest from each other.

The idea of affinity can, however, *operate* in different ways in the church; within the fundamental conviction common to both, the differences between the eastern and western churches on this matter are clear. And that common conviction can still take on all sorts of concrete-historical forms, which as such do not in any way detract from its universal unchangeable validity. The so-called "apostolic rule" (I deliberately said "so-called"): no marriage *after ordination,* is among others one of the most weighty "conclusions" drawn by the church from the theological idea of affinity. But still we should not lose sight of the ambiguous origin of this "ancient canon" of which the Council of Nicaea spoke. The Nicaean canon stems from a time when people thought of a "second marriage" as a kind of "respectable fornication."[1] In those days, most ordinands were already married when they became priests; to marry after ordination practically came down to the sort of second marriage so much scorned in the contemporary view. The "canon" originally—at least in its explicit intent —touched the priesthood only indirectly. The traditional

---

[1] See, for example, Athenagoras, *Supplicatio pro christianis* 33: *PG* 6, 965 and 968. The eastern church in particular judged more strictly on this point than the west. The presence of a priest at a second marriage was simply forbidden. See also Hippolytus, *Refutatio* IX, 12: *PG* 16, 3386. In present church law, "digamy" is still an "irregularitas ex defectu" for ordination (can. 984, n. 4). I would like to point out here that the book by D. S. Bailey, *The Man-Woman Relation in Christian Thought* (London 1959) has been taken too seriously. The substance of this book was taken in many respects from the already out-dated study of D. Lindner, *Der "usus matrimonii." Eine Untersuchung über seine sittliche Bewertung in der katholischen Moraltheologie alter und neuen Zeit,* Munich 1929. The author, writing in 1959, uncritically takes over facts from his 1929 source, including those relating to the authenticity of certain texts. Therefore on many points the historical perspective is completely distorted. Still, the book is an important source of information, at least for the *pejorative aspects* of ideas about marriage in the past.

interpretation which gave to 1 Tim 3:2 and Tit 1:6 ("the husband of one wife"), the significance of a prohibition for priests to re-marry, came just at that time when every "second marriage" was held to be unworthy.

In spite of this historically ambiguous origin, the eastern as well as the western church held strongly to this so-called "apostolic norm," even after the connection between it and the ancient depreciation of the second marriage had long since been lost. Of course, in the history of the church conclusions in many areas can often last for centuries after the premises on which they were based have disappeared. The *simple fact* that something has been going on for fifteen centuries in the church makes little impression upon a theologian. What matters is the significance of such a fact, and the insight that lies behind it. Sometimes as one looks back on it it seems senseless. But then this too has to be shown as meaningful, for the church itself does not exist only on insights that have already been "rationalised" or thematised, as the history of dogma concerning the sacraments and many other articles of faith clearly shows. Not to be allowed to marry after ordination has an evident theological connection with the *theological* idea of affinity, as an inadequate way of expressing the biblical experience of "existential inability to do otherwise."

But this fact has its unavoidable reactions on the psychology of the seminarian in training. One should not make sacramental ordination into a mystification, and therefore consider the priest's vocation as a whole. The theological affinity with celibacy "for the sake of the kingdom of

God" must be postulated of this vocation in its entirety. Then this affinity shows up *immediately*, not just after ordination, but from the moment a person makes himself a candidate for the priesthood and devotes himself to it as to a life commitment. Therefore, I personally do not see any difference in value and weight between the rule of "no marriage after ordination" (at least: together with the actual practice of the ministry) and the statement that "a seminarian may not marry." The one is the other, unless one wishes to make a mystification out of ordination as such. But in that case I am afraid that the ancient motive of "cultic purity" comes into play unconsciously.

Of course, one could be consistent in the opposite direction as well; that is, taking the statement "no marriage after ordination" as the one to be criticised. The *logical* consistency of this position cannot be denied. The question is whether we really get anywhere in matters of faith with logically cogent arguments alone; in our own times, just these forms of "logical conclusions" in theology have rightly been called into question. Given the real affinity between church ministry and religious celibacy—indeed the central point of the conciliar statement on clerical celibacy—we cannot accuse the hierarchy, who after all are the leaders of God's people, of going beyond their proper competence if they do require this bond for themselves and for priests, and therefore do not allow those already ordained to marry and still remain in office. Personally I have little sympathy for a church policy in which juridical rules in fact prevail over the impelling force of biblical inspiration. But in the whole of the church's life they can also be the juridical (and therefore unsympathetic) expression of the power of that sovereign invitation of the "ministry for the sake of the kingdom of God," and hence most sympathetic; for ministry in the church is by definition an offer of grace.

In the preceding chapter we tried to show how the *law* of celibacy is also meaningful in anthropological terms, but added that such a psychological pattern is ambivalent. If in the entirety of the church's life it should appear that this psychological pattern, normally speaking, is working in the wrong way and is even causing distress and disorder, then we ought to remember the first necessity: the people of God have a *right* to the ministry of their priests. This ecclesiological fact carries more weight than the church law of an unmarried priesthood. Unlike the west, the east sees the married priesthood as dictated by pastoral considerations. In no way should this be viewed as a second-rate kind of priesthood even though the church in principle grants the preference to clerical celibacy, in order to make the ministry *"for the sake of* the kingdom of God" into that striking eschatological sign. Just as I have pleaded elsewhere against a Christianity that looks upon itself as a superstructure built upon secular life, I feel equally obliged to emphasize the eschatological character of the church *ministry* and therefore also its connection with religious celibacy. But still, the psychological pattern, the dialectic between the "law of celibacy" and the focus upon the experience of "not being able to do otherwise," must also function normally.

When the psychological archetype of the fasting law and of the eucharistic fast began in reality to work adversely, the church did not cast them off but regulated them in another way. Thus in regard to the theological affinity between ministry and religious celibacy, I can only see the *abolition* of celibacy for priests as detrimental. Perhaps our own age, which thinks only of getting rid of things, is still not creative enough to fashion new forms in which the Christian relation between ministry and religious celibacy can *really* come to the fore. This creativity naturally requires cooperation among theologians (laymen and priests), teachers, social psychologists, sociologists, psychologists, psychiatrists, etc., and also with Christians of other faiths. But this common search must take place in a *Christian* way: in faith, and this is always a being-committed to the biblical experience of religious celibacy as "existential inability to do otherwise," which was in the first place the experience of the apostles who were caught up into the kingdom of God and their service to it.[2]

This whole problem is highly charged with emotion, which makes it difficult to approach calmly, even for those who are defending clerical celibacy. Their aggressiveness

---

[2] This experience need not be *per se* the intense experience of a single moment. Actually, it is a growth of perhaps several years. After Christ's "calling of the apostles," as the synoptics tell it ("and they followed him"), we often see them still "at home" and in the same circles where they were working before their calling. Although they were married before they had this experience, they did not go back to their family lives but on the contrary devoted themselves completely, and their wives also, to their ministerial work and daily assistance to the church (1 Cor 9:5).

seems to me to be as detrimental as the aggressiveness with which others attack it; this mutual explosiveness was certainly one of the reasons why public discussion was cut off at least in the council by orders from above. I am only pleading for the need for expert study of the subject, and concern for an integrated, humanly undamaged priestly life—but also, primarily and emphatically, for an awareness of the apostolic experience of the early church: the kingdom of God contains within itself an inner, objective quality which can be the origin of the inner conclusion that "existentially I cannot marry." This holds for *all* the faithful, but the *official* ministry of the kingdom of God— which as office is also charisma—contains in a special way the affinity with the charisma of the "being unmarriageable for the sake of the kingdom of God." If all the sociological, depth-psychological and psycho-hygienic studies of the celibacy question keep sight of this fact with its firm roots in the Bible and the authentic tradition of the church, then I have no fear for the future, whatever actual changes may follow from it. But I do fear for the secular expertise that is not guided by the Christian feeling for the biblical *eisin enuouchoi:* there are people who for the sake of the kingdom of God are unfit for married life. If this feeling is indeed present, then we can bank on the future, even if events may possibly turn out otherwise than we have been accustomed to traditionally.